I Am the Emperor

I Am the Emperor

I AM THE EMPEROR

Fill yourself up.
Get it all. Do it all.
All you want and need most.
This and only this, I believe, is the way we'll put behind us—
safely and forever—accelerating ecological ravage and the
threat of nuclear war.

Sandy Weymouth

The Anthony E. Weymouth Foundation, Inc.
P.O. Box 286
North East, MD 21901
www.thewoodsplace.com

I Am The Emperor/Sandy Weymouth. — 1st ed.
ISBN 9780997668902
ISBN: 0997668903

Contents

Introduction · ix

Part One Root · 1
Emotional Work· 3
External Absolutes · 15

Part Two Stem · 23
Logic of Life· 25
Technology · 35
Consumption · 45
Nuclear war · 63

Part Three Blossom · 75
Climax of technology 1 · 77
Climax of technology 2 · 89
Woods Place· 103
What If We Did? ·119

Part Four Seed · 131
Edith · 133
Wrap-up· 145
I Am The Emperor· 157
Dedications · 163

Introduction

Tangy stuff, right? Do it all? Get it all? Total self-gratification, total *greed*? Not what we were brought up on—not even the bad guys, I think.

This essay argues that total self-gratification is *the* principle of consciousness and behavior that will enable our species to circumvent finally and irreversibly the apocalyptic dangers we all wisely dread: gross and irreparable disruption of the Earth's ecology, nuclear war, breakdown of social and economic order, and general destruction of human and other life.

This essay argues that the history of life on Earth has reached its climax. At the climax of a life system, one species has developed the technical ability to destroy much, maybe all, of the life in that system. The tool in our case is nuclear weaponry. Also at the climax, this dominant species uses its burgeoning technological power to feed, entertain and otherwise serve itself exclusively, wiping out all plant, animal and other life that doesn't serve those purposes.

The essay argues that the very ways of thinking and behaving that have made this dominant, technological species so spectacularly successful must turn upside down so that the species' full power to alter and destroy is not realized. Only at and after the climax of life can a total self-gratification culture work. And from then on it's the only one that *will* work.

This book is about surrender. Surrendering up to the deepest parts of us. Feeling the deepest parts of us. And getting for ourselves what we want and need most deeply and most authentically. The book argues that we couldn't live that way in the past. And it argues that we must live that way now if our species is to continue to survive.

Do and get what you want and need most *now*, and experience the feelings that come up along the way. That's the standard, the ideal of consciousness and behavior that this book proposes.

The ravaging glutton within us is the very best part of us. I believe that, and I believe that now is the time for us to learn it. Surrender to the glutton, to the Emperor, the Empress, to the animal within, to whatever you want to call it. Do that and you'll do the world more good than you're doing it now. That's the argument of *I Am The Emperor*.

Part One
Root

EMOTIONAL WORK

Some years ago when I was 34, I got into emotional work. Very simple principle: experience your feelings. Yes, it can be helpful to look at them, analyze them, think and talk about them, express them in some way. But if you really want to do something about them, feel them. As deeply and completely as possible.

Rarely a day goes by that I don't spend time surrendering to feelings. Not acting on them necessarily. Humans may be unique in their ability to separate the experience of feelings from action those feelings can provoke. It's my experience that surrendering to feelings and letting them do what they want to do inside you reduces pressure to do things that might generate new and worse feelings.

I spend time most days experiencing feelings, often in bed before I get up. I'm curled up, surrendering, just feeling whatever it is---anxiety, impotence, inferiority, guilt at lying around in bed. Occasionally I put myself in a place where I can be fairly uninhibited---cars with all the windows up are great for this. If my feelings seem out of reach, I experience them as that: out of reach. But in a closed car on a lonely lane or even at the far end of a parking lot, I can scream if I want. Pain, rage, fear, anything. For me, screaming usually becomes cathartic gut-coughing, climaxing with a cleansing wad of phlegm thrown from deep inside.

Sometimes I cry. That's hard for me. But when it comes, it's the kind of torrential washing and emptying that happened when I was little. Sometimes I scream joy and power, how great I feel. How great I am!

The result is a changed consciousness. The feelings—even guilt, anxiety and depression—have shifted or dissipated. I'm freer to act, to do what I need to do. What I need to do seems clearer. I'm energized, mobilized. I feel good.

When I face working on this book after time away from it, I get cottonhead. Wet cotton. Horizonless anxiety, numb despair, I don't have anything to say, I couldn't say it if I did, I'm under a sandbag the size of a house. What I do is go to my beloved old brown Corolla. There I surrender. The last time I did this, last night, the groggy, impotent feeling changed to something positive. Maybe I can. Maybe I can do it (the book). I came back, I wrote, and here I am.

The effect doesn't last. But continued emotional work has a cumulative effect. It's clear to me that feelings are *the* mechanism by which organisms respond to their environment. Worms, plant cells, algae all experience pleasure, pain, maybe even fear. Feelings teach organisms how things in their environment will affect them and what actions will best enable them to survive. Feelings show me my next step and how to take it. I learn whether the last step was best, or whether the best step now is back where I was before—or even back beyond that. Back is the best step forward sometimes.

Everybody "experiences their feelings," you say—more than they want to. That's the point, say I. They experience their feelings more than they want to, so they do all kinds of things to stop feeling them or feel them less. Surrendering to feelings just isn't something we're conditioned to do. So what do you do? How do you do it?

I've mentioned some of the things I do. A tidal wave of rage will get me in my car where I bellow for all I'm worth. Usually vital to this is deep coughing climaxing with cathartic goop. Sorry, it works for me. Sometimes I scream pain. Same result usually.

At the other end of the catharsis spectrum, I periodically wake early in the morning, 3, 4 o'clock, feeling inert, inadequate, I'm an embryo, void of motivation, virtually void of life. Surrendering to these feelings draws me into a fetal position on my left side, to a corridor of energy that starts on the left side of my chest and goes up to the center of my head. When I fully surrender to this inertness, this catatonia, something seems to percolate through this corridor. Energy goes from one place to another, and after a while I feel different. My mind goes to things in the outside world and I'm usually up and functioning without having consciously decided to be.

Is this what you should do? Scream your head off? Cough up goop? Curl up like a fetus and let void energy percolate up your corridor? Damned if I know. The trick is to do something other than ignore or suppress feelings that come up. To feel them completely—not just enough to know they're there.

Emotional work is a new game, I think. Not much is known about the specifics. I don't know whether you have a "corridor" or, if you do, whether it's in the same place as mine. People may have different ways and means of processing feelings. Or they may not. One friend of mine needs to be extremely violent, to hit, slam and kick violently where he won't do anyone or thing, himself included, any harm—on a wrestling mat, for example. Matter of fact, I like doing that myself.

Be careful about translating your feelings to behavior, to outward action. There are laws, and as you'll see later, my exhorting you to do emotional work is not an exhortation to violate or abolish laws or community customs and mores. These will change in time. They always have.

The key is to experiment with the faith that the deepest, most authentic parts of you are perfect. They can't harm you or others, human or otherwise. They don't want to. They're perfect. *That's* the faith.

I got into emotional work in New York after a friend dared me to try the Casriel Institute. My life needed something, I was shopping around for a psychotherapist, and it seemed my friend had achieved much at Casriel in a short time. My first indication of what Casriel was about came while sitting in the dingy first floor waiting room of the Institute, a townhouse near St. Patrick's Cathedral. I was early for a "beginners group," so I was alone. From overhead erupted a mass scream like what must have been heard under the Coliseum when they told the Christians they were on in five. I almost snuck out.

In the beginners group were a couple of plants—people who, when it came their turn to talk, fell right into cathartic screaming and sobbing. This moved me. These people weren't beginners, but they weren't phonies either. I immediately had tremendous feelings for them and for what they were doing. A big burly guy sobbed in Dan Casriel's arms about Daddy. Dan was the psychiatrist who ran the Institute and was leading this group. At the end, he lead us in a group scream. I always think of the Exorcist girl when I remember the next several minutes. I didn't throw up any green stuff, but I bent forward and hissed—-we were all holding hands at this point—-this guttural, wordless venom. Anger I guess, lots of it. I stopped way after everyone else. Dan looked on with approval: he had a live one.

I floated out of the Institute on a carpet of euphoria that lasted for hours, maybe days. I went once or twice a week to the Institute for the next year or so, with good Merck, the pharmaceutical manufacturer and my employer, paying 80 percent of the freight. If they hadn't, I probably would have weaseled out.

Occasionally I saw someone individually, but usually I went to groups lead either by Dan, a woman named Frankie Wiggin who was tremendous at cooking up pandemonium, or Parks Wightman. Parks, the wild man of the operation, had a complicated falling out with Dan and had to leave a year or so after I started. A number of us went with him. Parks had no credentials, so no more Merck coverage. But Parks was cheaper. Dan and Parks were in their early fifties then; Frankie was younger.

Early on in this whole experience, one thought emerged clearly in my mind that has stayed clear ever since. What really made the difference in these groups was emotional work. Dan, Frankie and Parks did a lot of attitude work along with emotional work. To me, the two are entirely different.

Attitude work, as I see it, undertakes to fortify a person with an "attitude," often a slogan, a way of thinking about things, a verbalized approach to life that you keep in your hip pocket as a general guide for when things get rough. Then you bring it out, remember it, and use it to get through the rough situation. One of the earliest things I remember Dan saying was "Just tell 'em, if you can get it up, you can have it." ("Get my male member up," he's saying.) Sounded like the special of the week. Lots of impotence around, and Dan loved his new weapon: dump the responsibility on somebody else.

I loved Dan and I love his idea. But the idea I love better is: surrender totally to the impotence feelings and any others that might be underneath them.

Frankie would feed you lines. In her groups, after you had talked about what was on your mind for a while, she'd say something like "Just tell your father 'I don't have to perform to get your love.'" You'd resist this and say it was stupid and you didn't want to do it, and Frankie'd ask you when you're going to learn that your way didn't work, and other group members would egg you on, and you'd talk and talk and maybe scream and holler and swear very loud. But finally, you'd murmur okay and after a long silence you'd look at each group member one by one and say "I don't have to perform to get your love," seeing in each face your father, of course. We sat in folding chairs around third-hand, faintly greasy wrestling mats you could go berserk on when you wanted to. Groups usually had six to ten people. Sometimes they were larger. Dan often held weekend workshops or marathons involving fifty to a hundred people. They were great.

So, around the circle you'd go. "I don't have to perform to get your love. I don't have to perform to get *your* love." You'd say it and say it, maybe going around the circle several times, and then something would start to connect and you'd get louder and louder and start screaming and then scream other things that came to mind and then just scream. A-A-A-A-AH. And maybe you'd get really hot and leap on the mattress and kick and bang with your fists and by now everybody else who'd been egging you on is screaming their own stuff and banging and kicking and thrashing around on the floor. "JUST GO CRAZY!" Parks would yell when things got like this in his groups. These were adults, you understand.

It was great. Each of these therapists was great. Dan and Parks are gone, Dan of Lou Gehrig's Disease in 1982, Parks of cancer in 1984. Frankie, I heard, is leading groups in Florida. They all generated tremendous energy in their groups and their individual work, and they all put tremendous emphasis on getting into and blowing out feelings, loud and wild. And I'm convinced this had great therapeutic effect for many people, notably me.

However, the credo that emerged in my head as a result of this experience is different, as I see it, from much of what Dan, Frankie and Parks did. Credo: unexperienced feelings are what keep us down. I believe unexperienced feelings keep a heavily medicated psychiatric patient from being free of medication and as mentally healthy as most people; I believe they keep the world's most successful business people, artists and leaders from being supermen and superwomen. And I believe that unexperienced feelings immensely aggravate all physical and mental disorders, including birth-related brain damage, autism and other congenital retardation.

And the one comprehensive way to treat unexperienced feelings is to experience them. Feel them. They're our oldest, most potent tools for adaptation. When we allow them to operate freely, we adapt, move and grow. That's how they work. That's what they're there for.

And experiencing all feelings completely, I argue, is precisely what *every* human culture in the past has committed itself to preventing. They had to. We today are different. We're living at the climax of life on Earth. We no longer have to keep ourselves from experiencing our feelings. But we do anyway. And we use hosts of aids and techniques to "relieve"—i.e. suppress—feelings that present the slightest discomfort. And we give each other enormous support for doing it. An ethos of feelings suppression permeates our surroundings and comes at us from virtually everything that talks.

At Casriel and even with Parks, I became frustrated seeing attitude work in a process I thought was grounded in something bigger. I was frustrated when I saw someone present a slogan, an attitude, a way of thinking to someone else as a way of dealing with a problem or with life. So many sentences started with "Just tell yourself" or "You've just got to realize that..."

Parks loved aphorisms. They were the principal vehicle for his wisdom, which I think was prodigious. He looked a little like Ho Chi Minh, only longer, scrawnier and more scraggly-bearded. His aphorisms were funny and their off-the-wallness made them liberating.

Only five words needed for communication, he claimed: No, Stop, Help, More, Now. Tips on getting laid included "stumble and drool power," which always came with a short demonstration. Parks was expert at drooling and saying "dah-h." Works every time, he claimed: takes the pressure off performing and being cool. Two Parksisms I particularly love: we rarely forgive those whom we hurt; and to really accept is to accept that we are not accepted. Here's another: obsessions are great. I love that.

I loved his aphorisms and so did many others. But the fact of the aphorisms ran against the fact of emotional work, which Parks also did as skillfully as I've seen it done. He loved to get people into their feelings. He loved noise. He believed that getting in deep, long and loud is *the* potent healer.

But to me, emotional work, by orienting you to what *you* feel, orients you to what *you* think, to *your* adaptation to the world. Aphorisms, no matter how funny, off-the-wall and liberating, orient you to what somebody else thinks, how somebody else has adapted and is adapting to the world.

Don't get me wrong. Attitude work has a long history of success. Anthropologists tell us that literacy, the ability to use words, goes back millions of years and several humanoid species. It seems likely to me that as soon as people could talk, they started telling each other what to think and do. Attitude work, I'm convinced, has existed in all verbal cultures and, therefore, could be millions of years old.

Mothers, fathers, medicine-men, priests, wise men, prophets, philosophers, political leaders and corporate consultants, either in their proselytizing, in requested counsel, or in compulsory teaching, have told people what and how to think, how to look at things and what to do about them. Trust in God, think positive thoughts, stiff upper lip, never say die, one day at a time, I don't have to perform to get your love, cleanse your mind of all worldly thoughts. How many times have you heard "Your attitude's all wrong; your attitude should be...." And then there's "You shouldn't feel that way." Mouth foams as I write that one.

Part of the message of attitude work is inevitably *don't* feel your feelings. Even Parks believed people shouldn't feel guilty. I say: feel guilty? Feel guilty. *Really* guilty. Give up to it totally. Best way in the world to resolve it and get rid of it. Depressed? Sink into it. Deep as it goes. It's there for a reason. Suppressing the feeling, particularly with the help of mood-altering substances—caffeine, nicotine, alcohol, and over-the-counter, prescription and illegal drugs—all these jam and impact, like a wisdom tooth, the reason for the feeling. Experience the feeling and you reveal the reason it's there. Free the impacted tooth of wisdom and let it out!

Attitude work is about teaching, counseling and proselytizing. Getting inside somebody else's head and changing the wiring. Steering them right. I.e., steering them where *you* think is right. Away from where *they* think is right.

In its purest form, emotional work doesn't teach, counsel or proselytize anything. Not even to do emotional work. Emotional work waits for openings. Opportunities to get behind people, get behind their feeling, thinking, saying and doing what they want to feel, think, say and do. Opportunities to validate *them*, the people, not ideas, particularly somebody else's ideas.

Am I violating my own creed? Writing this book? Telling you to experience your feelings? Telling you to do and get what you want and need most? Maybe. Am I telling you to read the book? Stop reading the Goddamn book. Do what you want to do most. Now. Writing the book's what *I* want to do most now.

Emotional work is more than a therapy. It's a way to interact. When it's authentic, when it's the only way we want to interact—not because I say so, not because it's the good way, the right way, but because it *feels* best, it's the most fun—then I think you've got the optimum. Optimal personal interaction. They'll never find a better way for organisms to interact than that.

Let other people—even our children—make their mistakes. They learn more by discovering than by being taught. More and better. We'll cover the toddler who wants to toddle the freeway. And the folks who want to molest children and eliminate races of humanity. But use the toddler to justify controls, manipulations and "I know what's best for you," do that and you're missing the boat, I think. You're making life a thousand times harder and the rewards a thousand times less than what's possible. For you *and* the toddler.

You may have doubts—I don't—that from every point of view man has come a long way since he became verbal. And counseling, teaching and preaching—attitude work—has been essential to that progress. It couldn't have happened without it. Force, no doubt, played a big part, *making* people think and act the way a community's ruling consensus wanted them to: love Jesus or burn. Like it or not, that too was part of humanity's success.

For eons, attitude work has disseminated the adaptation that was working for the social organism, be it family, tribe, kingdom or nation-state. Stiff upper lip and never say die worked for Britain and Empire. The cultural values they bespoke enabled the English to realize the enormous possibilities of a lucky geography. Limp upper lip, die sometimes maybe, and some other culture would have realized those possibilities.

Natural selection picks the winners and losers among all organisms, including human cultures. And attitude work—preaching, teaching, and coercing—has disseminated the adaptation, has gotten the word around within those cultures, winners *and* losers. Whether or not a culture's competitive strategy for survival succeeded, attitude work is what disseminated the strategy among the members, new members for example.

So what makes things different now? What invalidates attitude work all of a sudden? Technology does. The clock of human history. Technology alone determines the nature and timing of change in human history, I believe. And when the clock says that a species' technology can wipe out virtually all of that species and *is* wiping out rapidly increasing quantities of others, it's time for a change. The great irony of our age—the age of the climax—is that what always worked in the past is precisely what *won't* work now.

In the apocalyptically dangerous game of the climax, control is the route to failure, while fill-her-up-all-the-way/total self-gratification is the route to success. The precise logic of this belief I want to save until Part 3.

And emotional work—doing and getting all of what you want and need most and experiencing the feelings that come up along the way—emotional work heals and promotes growth faster and more completely than any kind of attitude work or anything else, if there *is* anything else. That's my conviction. What works best for the individual works best for the species—at least now and in the future it does. If this is the case, aren't we lucky? Aren't we lucky that doing and getting all of what each of us wants and needs most is *the* way past the horrific perils of our life system's climax.

Somebody or thing will make it past the climax eventually. If we blow it, life will keep on going. We don't have the power to destroy it all. Not yet. And either remnants of our species or some new species will evolve with the same powers we have now. Maybe they'll blow it too. But somebody or something will make it someday, and emotional work and what it's about is how I think they'll do it.

Me, I don't want to leave it for some species or some remnant down the road to get past. I, the Emperor, want to get past now. *This* time. *This* round. That's why I'm writing this book. Save the world. Why not?

External Absolutes

Life could be a dream. Everything I see, hear, touch, all of it could be a dream, a fabulous movie put on by some unimaginable agency for some unimaginable reason. Not an original thought. You've thought this, I'm sure—assuming you exist. Maybe I'm schizophrenic: maybe there's a real world out there, but what I think I'm doing and what I think is happening in the real world just isn't the case. Fevered delirium, hallucination. It could be that.

Emotional work helped me on this, by orienting me to what I feel. No illusions there. If I feel afraid or depressed or confused or just messed up, is somebody going to tell me I'm wrong? That's *not* the way I feel? Maybe I don't know how I feel. Is somebody going to tell me I *do* know? Even if I'm schizophrenic, or it's all hallucination or the fabulous movie, I'm feeling it. That's certain. That's rock solid.

Same with what I perceive: and by what I perceive I mean sounds, tastes, anything that could have gotten into my consciousness through any of the senses, not just the visual. The point is, my perceptions may *not* have gotten into my consciousness through my senses. They may have generated spontaneously in my consciousness. Or maybe God sent them: visions, voices. Maybe they're drug-induced, or the result of acute loneliness, isolation or fear. But no matter where they come from, my perceptions are in my consciousness. No illusions there, either. I can't be certain of what's really out there in the real world, assuming it's out there at all. But I can always be certain of what I perceive. The sights, sounds, smells, etc. in my consciousness, no matter how they got in here, are rock solid.

Same with thinking. What I'm thinking may be muddled, undefined, unclear, vague, mixed-up, stupid, crazy or disordered. But can there be any doubt to me that I'm thinking it? Is it conceivable that I'm not thinking what I think I'm thinking? That I'm really thinking something else? It's not conceivable to me. We're talking conscious thought here. Sure, we could argue all day about what I'm "thinking unconsciously." Let's not.

I know what I feel, perceive and think. I don't think there's anything else I can know with the same certainty. I don't know if there's a God, I don't know what's important, I don't know what kind of behavior is "appropriate," I don't know what I *ought* to do, what's right, wrong, good, bad, and I don't know what the truth is, what the "facts" are. I may have strong opinions on these matters—you're reading a book full of them. But I know nothing for certain about any of them. I *do* know what I feel, perceive and think, without a glimmer of doubt.

Then again, maybe I *don't* know. Maybe I get confused about what I feel, perceive and think. Maybe it's all uncertain or vague sometimes, or all the time. But there's no doubt about the absolute truth of the confusion, uncertainty or vagueness. They are absolute, while God, "appropriate" and truth are not. Not for me anyway.

I think most of us spend our lives worrying and arguing over what's "objectively" right, wrong, true, false, normal, abnormal, sick, healthy, attractive and tacky. We orient ourselves, we orient what we think and say, to "objective reality," to facts, to absolutes, or The Absolute, to *the truth*.

I call these external absolutes. They're facts. And they're outside our individual consciousnesses. I think the only real facts are *inside* our individual consciousnesses. No, the only *real* facts are inside *my* consciousness. *My* feelings, perceptions and thoughts. If you really exist, then I'd think the only real facts for you are in *your* consciousness, *your* feelings, perceptions and thoughts.

We worry and argue about external absolutes because we're looking for them. We're sure they're out there, but we haven't found a way to determine which ones or One is the real thing. So we worry and argue and look and look and look. Is it God, Muhammad, Buddha? Universal Mind, Cosmic Energy, Chi? The alternative to all this worrying, arguing and looking, I think, is to orient oneself to one's own personal point of view, to one's feelings and perceptions. Me Me Me. Now we're talking rocks, the stuff of absolute knowledge.

External absolutes versus personal point of view. Which orientation is really true, rock solid and reliable may be an engaging matter to contemplate. What's more important to me, though, is the corrosive effect which I think external absolutes have on the strength and vigor of the individual psyche—the ego, the consciousness—and on the quality of human interaction.

A friend of mine who for most of his adult life has been going to psychiatrists, psychotherapists, groups, nutritionists, psychics, rebirthings and, for a while, me, worries about whether his thinking is distorted. Where's the book on undistorted? Who decides what's distorted and what isn't? If it's a consensus within the psychiatric community, fine: personal opinion of one or many on distorted thinking. But my friend doesn't perceive his distortions as the opinion of some individual or group. He perceives them as fact, the truth.

So what? Truth or opinion, what difference does it make? I can only speak subjectively: *my* perception of my friend's consciousness. I experience him as feeling more lonely, isolated, immobilized, inferior, confused and hopeless—more than he'd feel were his distorted thinking more generally presented as somebody's personal opinion. I see him facing a taller, more judgmental, more scornful universe, filled with people whose *un*distorted thinking is fact, people who are better than he is.

An opinion, on the other hand, is one human speaking to another. It's a person dropping trou a little, exposing himself, giving something of his own. Paradoxically, I find the drop-trou kind of communication a great defense. It reduces the burden of proof. It's my opinion, my experience, what's to prove? It's so easy to speak confidently about what you know. And as I say, the only thing I really know is what I feel, perceive and think.

External absolutes hurt people, unnecessarily, I think. We tie our egos, our identities, to our external absolutes—to our politics, religion, friends, car, neighborhood, clothes, books, diet, movies, rock groups and on and on. Then we argue and fight over them. And it's in verbal wars where egos get hurt. Why hurt an ego? Talk personal opinions and there's nothing to fight about. You exchange opinions, you don't wield them.

Maybe I've had heavy external absolutes like "distorted thinking" dumped on me, but it's the less personal ones that I remember throwing me off. Facts that I didn't know about or didn't agree with. Facts that made me feel inferior, alone, way behind and hopeless of ever catching up.

Walter Bagehot, the most original mind of his generation. Microwave ovens are unnatural. Stevie Wonder is a genius. Pornography degrades women. Lutèce, the greatest restaurant in America. And then there's Lutèce, *probably* the greatest restaurant in America. Use "probably" when you want your statement of fact to sound sober, considered, balanced. *Probably* the phoniest adverb in our language.

Facts. The thing is, I don't know who Walter Bagehot is; I like pornography—or erotica anyway—and Stevie Wonder seems like a wonderful person, but I don't get his music. Organic New Age Hippie Earth People live on external absolutes; it's one thing that makes them so damned bourgeois to me. "Microwaves put the wrong kind of energy in food." Says who? Bhagwan Shree Rajneesh? Well, he's entitled to his opinion, of course. The problem is, it's not a matter of opinion: "Microwave ovens are unnatural" *is*. The statement is truth, one with the cosmic energy, eternal, even though microwave ovens are not. How did this truth get to us? Who, what revealed it how? That's what I want to know!

I have a life history of buying into external absolutes. They make me feel alienated, inadequate, inferior. I'm up in my room, the party's going on downstairs, and nobody misses me. I must read everything by Walter Bagehot and by everybody else in his generation he was more original than, listen critically to the entire opus of Stevie Wonder, research the entire literature on microwaves and eat everything at every restaurant so I can be *sure* Lutèce is the best. And shame, shame, shame. Burn that degrading pornography. Get into things that are healthy wholesome normal natural.

I like boys better than girls. This, of course, runs me up against one of the most deeply impacted external absolutes in our culture, the more so since AIDS. "I hate faggots." I have no problem with that. On the contrary, I dig it. In an emotional work context, I totally support somebody shrieking it while pulverizing mattresses and pillows with a crow-bar (safe distance, of course). My belief is: the louder the bellows and the more chewed up foam rubber in the air, the sooner us faggots get a new ally. If not, it doesn't matter. Regardless of the outcome, I support hating faggots. It's a personal feeling. And I support personal feelings totally.

But start a sentence with "Faggots are" and I get bent. You're stating a fact there, not a personal feeling or opinion. "You've got to make up your mind," counseled a woman I went out with years ago. "Boys or girls." You've got to make up your mind, SAYS WHO? If she was speaking for herself, fine. One sexuality at a time's all she can handle? No problem. But she wasn't speaking for herself, I think. She was speaking for Womankind, for Normal and Natural, for Grown Up. She was talking external absolutes, and I didn't like it.

Trying to legitimize my opinions by tying them to any absolute other than my own personal consciousness, my own thoughts, feelings and perceptions, is, I think, a tricycle trip to nowhere. There are no good books, beautiful paintings or transcendent symphonies. What a liberation it was to discover this, or decide it. There are no standards. None. Except the ones we make up. There are books, paintings and symphonies that have turned me and, apparently, huge numbers of other people on hugely.

It's a relative universe we live in. Relative because we all take in, process and interact with different parts of it in different ways at different times and speeds. We can handle relativity in physics; let's get it into our language, our consciousnesses, into our experience of our relative environments and realities. Here's a personal opinion: objectivity's a fake. Here's a personal directive: surrender to your subjectivity. This is the Emperor talkin'.

God. You can't talk external absolutes and not talk God. The definitive external absolute. My objection to the way most construe God is the same as my objection to external absolutes. God is a basis for telling me what to feel, think, say and do.

Many homosexuals argue that the Bible doesn't call homosexuality a sin. So what if it doesn't? Those homosexuals are buying into the external absolute. Only they claim the external absolute is *not* telling them what they don't want to hear. I don't care what the Bible says about homosexuality. What tells me the Bible is anything more than the feelings, experience and opinions of some people living a very long time ago? What tells me the Bible wasn't written by very primitive people whom, if we could somehow meet them, we'd find as alien as contemporary primitive people?

What authenticates the Bible? Faith? Fine. I certainly have faiths. Faiths that I can't support with much in the way of logic or empirical data, have you noticed? But faiths are subjective, I think. The only thing is, they're thought of and communicated as absolutes. No one ever tells me it's their *faith* homosexuality is a sin. It's a sin. Period. Fact.

Now there's no logical contradiction I can see between believing in God and believing that my consciousness now is the only thing I can be certain of. God just doesn't get to be an external absolute any more. You believe in him, but you're just not certain about him the way you're certain about what you feel, perceive and think.

Perfectly reasonable arrangement, it seems to me, and one God wouldn't need to get sore about. I mean, if he's got any brains at all, he'd have to acknowledge that a consciousness can be certain only of its feelings, perceptions and thoughts. Nothing more. Not God or anything else. It's a limitation of the mechanism. After all, how can God be sure it isn't all a movie put on for *him* by some unimaginable agency for some unimaginable reason?

Me Me Me. The Me Generation. The most promising cultural development of our time. *My* feelings. *My* perceptions. *My* thoughts. What *I* need, what *I* want. The fallout from this orientation will be different, I believe, from what we've trained ourselves to expect. Me Me Me is the starting point for optimal consciousness and optimal personal interaction, the best kind of consciousness and behavior—the most profoundly and copiously generous, for example—that will ever emerge, in humans or any species. And it's a cultural development that runs dead against the deepest, most successful values of our civilization: self-discipline, self-restraint, self-denial—which all boil down to self-distrust.

We need something out there to guide us. We need external absolutes. Or so we've thought. And we were probably right. I believe that external absolutes—like attitude work—were essential to the bounding success of the human species. It would have been impossible without them.

But the game's changed. We're at the climax of history. From now on, the values and standards that made us great will destroy us. Turn them upside down. Do the Apocalyptic Back Flip. We *must* execute the apocalyptic back flip *or else*. Because it's Right. It's the Moral, Noble thing to do, the Sacrifice that will Save Us. Right? Wrong. We *will* execute the apocalyptic back flip because it's what we want to do most. Because it's the sexiest, funnest thing to do. Why? How? Let's talk about that now.

Part Two
Stem

LOGIC OF LIFE

In her 1982 book *Early Life*, biologist Lynn Margulis describes various steps of evolution prior to the appearance of multicellular organisms. Each of these steps saved life—not just lives, all of life—because the organisms involved used resources more efficiently or otherwise developed flexibility or power their predecessors didn't have. In all her marvelous book, I quibble with only one sentence, near the end: "It would be a misreading of the evolutionary record to think of these events as a kind of upward progression." Increased flexibility, increased power, increased efficiency in resource use, that's what every microstep of evolution produced. It had to, or it wouldn't have been a microstep of evolution. And look what it lead to: *us*. Humans who can observe, classify and maybe even understand this stuff. Humans and their (I think) constantly expanding consciousnesses. Sounds like progress to me.

As I see it, where life is involved, progress is a logical necessity. No alternative. It's a deterministic universe we live in, and I'm not talking God's plan, karma, must-have-been-something-he-did-in-a-former-life crap. It's a universe driven by logic: mechanistic, one-billiard-ball-knocking-another logic. It's the only way any universe *can* work. It's built into the meaning of universes. *I* think it is.

In MIT physicist Alan H. Guth's model of the origin of the universe, one of the hot ones among such models, everything—not just all matter and energy, but all space and time—came from virtually nothing. Absolutely nothing, maybe. "Not readily grasped by human intuition," scientists like to say about stuff like this. I'll say. Imagine nothing. Not even empty space, time, anything. And then imagine the universe popping out of it.

Guth traces it all back to the first 100 nonillionth of a second. A 100 nonillionth is 100000000000000000000000-00000001. Thirty-one zeros. Starting then, the universe entered what Guth calls the "inflationary era," a period of rapid expansion lasting several 100 nonillionths of a second at least. Short era, but a lot happened. During the first second of the universe's life—or renewed life, could be either says Guth—the universe's radius expanded from one septendecillionth of a centimeter (don't you love these numbers? 53 zeros in this one— 00000000000000000000000000000000000000000000000000001," virtually" nothing wouldn't you agree?) the universe's radius expanded from one septendecillionth of a centimeter to oh say 600 trillion or so miles or about 106 light years. Some era, some inflation, some second. The ultimate free lunch, Guth likes to call it.

Guth's model is more than an inspired flight of the imagination, though it's certainly that. Much more than any other model so far, Guth's—when mathematically projected, when *logically* projected— results in a universe like the one we live in today.

The belief that the universe and all that happens in it is logical under-lies all scientific inquiry. When scientists ask why, I think they assume the answer will reveal (1) why what happened happened the way it did, (2) why it couldn't have happened any other way, and (3) why, because it could happen, it had to happen.

What can must. If conditions are right for an origin of a universe, Bang, Universe. It's gotta be. If it doesn't happen, not all the conditions were right. (I'll let the physicists and New Age cosmologists fight over how it could happen if there weren't any conditions at all.)

If conditions are right for all the stuff that's blown out in a cosmic Big Bang to aggregate into lumps—galaxies, stars, planets, etc.—that's what's going to happen. Scientists presume this when they ask why. Why didn't it all move out in an even spray? Why did it glob up?

Same with life. If conditions allow the formation of life—and there may be billions of kinds of conditions that do—if one kind exists, life must form. No choice. If it doesn't, something's missing.

And apparently life didn't waste any time occurring on Earth. The age of the earliest fossils yet found is about 3.5 billion years, putting them in the first quarter of the Earth's history. And those fossils—prokaryotes, the simpler of the two kinds of cells found on Earth—are complex enough to have required tens, maybe hundreds of millions of years to evolve. And go back only 11 hundreds of millions of years and you're at the formation of the Earth from gas and dust. So, conditions are go for life, life gets going, pronto. It has to. Logic requires it.

Reproduction is a dynamo of logic. Where there's reproduction, there has to be evolution and natural selection. No choice. But reproduction must involve three things. First, what's reproduced must be a little different from the original, at least every so often. If an entity can replicate only its exact duplicate, then there's no room for change, for evolution. Second, what's reproduced can't be too different from the original. If it is, some improvement that somehow happens along very likely won't get passed on to succeeding generations. And third, what's reproduced must be able in turn to reproduce. If not, obviously you don't have reproduction anymore.

Reproduction like this virtually requires life not only to occur but to elaborate into the unimaginable complexity it has become on

Earth. University of Glasgow chemist A. G. Cairns-Smith believes life might have started from clay crystals that evolve in water. The crystals might have become increasingly complex because a kind of molecule once alien to a given crystal might attach to a crystal cell and thereby alter that cell's structure. Duplicates of this altered crystal cell that would form around it would then need the same kind of once-alien molecule to be complete. In this way the character of the growing crystal structure would change.

The ringmaster, even at this early stage, is natural selection, the *logic* of natural selection. Crystal structures best adapted to their environment—temperature and movement of the water for example—survive and grow best.

The big break comes when some alien molecule attaching to a crystal cell causes the cell to separate from the rest of the crystal. But the separated crystal cell continues to pick up needed molecules to form a duplicate of itself. And once the duplicate is formed, it too breaks off from the original the way the first one did and starts forming a duplicate of its own. What a jump: independent complexes of molecules that successively replicate themselves. Alien molecules that attach to these independent self-replicators *and* that improve their adaptation to their environment make them progressively more complex so that eventually they acquire the structures and functions of life forms. You didn't like gorillas for kin, how do you like clay?

Why can't we see this happening today? Because the life the clay generated would beat the clay in competition for those "alien" molecules. Thanks for the lift, clay, now piss off. Nobody said natural selection was polite.

Logic. It seems to me logic would dictate the order in which all the various characteristics of life first appear, Earth or anywhere, this or any universe. The very process of crystal cells picking up needed molecules to form duplicates might have elaborated into all the metabolic processes, into picking up matter and energy from the environment, distributing and using it, and disposing of the waste.

But before this development could get far, you'd need some kind of envelope to keep increasingly sophisticated structures and processes from floating away from a little self-replicator. Inside such an envelope, an evolving metabolic process could really develop some sophistication. It could, for example, extract from consumed molecules energy that would enable a self-replicator to move.

Motility this is called, as opposed to mobility which can mean move or *be* moved. If you're motile, you move yourself. And if you're highly evolved, you can move and *not* move. And when you're really hip, you get to decide where you move and at what speed. No joke, evolving organisms must have gone through all these stages.

So now that you can move, wouldn't the ability to *feel* come in handy? Before, it would have been useless. What use would feeling be if you couldn't do anything about what you felt? If you couldn't move? But possibly self-replicators *could* feel before they could move, even though the ability to feel didn't do them any good. Here's the reasoning.

Imagine you're an independent self-replicator that can both move and feel. So what? So nothing. The abilities to move and feel need a bridge, something remotely comparable to a thought process, maybe just a chemical reaction, something that converts awareness of, say, food or excess heat into movement to get the food or get out of the heat. Without this link to the ability to move, the ability to feel is useless.

So say self-replicators could move but not feel. If the ability to feel somehow appeared in one self-replicator, it would disappear in succeeding generations. Why? Because it's useless. There's no link between it and the ability to move. And a self-replicator having the ability to feel would presumably have to eat more matter and energy to sustain whatever mechanism enabled it to feel. This would put him at a disadvantage against competitors who could survive without eating as much.

But suppose some ability to feel were intrinsic to the replicating process, the way I've said the metabolizing process might have been. (I'll speculate in a few paragraphs on how the ability to feel might have been intrinsic to the replicating process.) Then when a self-replicator came along that could move, it would have both abilities which successions of offspring would pass on indefinitely: the ability to move because it gives a clear advantage over those that can't, and the ability to feel because it's been there all along. With these two abilities locked together in place, the needed link between the two could take its sweet time evolving.

Feelings. Sweet sweet feelings. I think sensory contact with the environment, even in the most primitive organisms, *is* feelings. It has emotional meaning, like pain or pleasure. No such thing as neutral sensation. Microbes in water that move toward light do so, I think, because the light feels good, not just because they're programmed to do it.

Pain, fear, anger, need, pleasure. These often came up at the Casriel Institute and with Parks as *the* five feelings which all the other things we call feelings boil down to. All organisms experience at least some of these feelings. Whole plants may not feel need, pain and pleasure, but their constituent cells do, I bet, depending on whether they're getting enough nutrition or are being traumatized in some way.

While there's little scientific basis for the above quintet of feelings, I buy them because they fit so nicely with the elemental experience of organisms. The charge in the evolving clay crystal that attracted and held molecules while forming a new crystal cell could be an electro-chemical "need." Conceivably, this was the basis of the need later experienced by organisms. Doesn't hunger, for example, originate as an electro-chemical need in the molecules of our cells? Similarly, the electro-chemical "satisfaction" of having those molecules just clunk! lock into place in the crystal could have been the basis of satisfaction and pleasure. (This is how these two feelings might have been intrinsic to the replicating process, as speculated above.)

After a sensory system developed some sophistication, pain could have told an organism things weren't going right. Later, fear could have developed as an ability to anticipate pain, motivating the organism to try to avoid it. Finally, some organisms might have experienced anger, both as an additional defense against pain and to intensify motivation to gratify need.

Once you've got something that can reproduce, metabolize, move and feel, you've got life. You could argue you had it earlier. Now it's definite.

And if you've got life, you've got competition. Again, it's a logical necessity. Life virtually means competition. Anything that replicates has to consume molecules to make the replicate of itself. And if it replicates, the number of things like it grows, while whatever it eats diminishes. (Replicators aren't eating other replicators yet, we're coming to that.) So whoever's got more of what it takes to get food—speed, strength, maybe just luck—eats and proliferates while others eat and proliferate less. Maybe not at all. Logic. Organisms survive in trillions of radically different ways. But they—we—all compete. Holy men of India compete, I think.

And sooner or later the supply of those tasty molecules that the earliest organisms were competing for, which do *not* replicate, has to run out. Food crisis. For which, ultimately, there's only one answer.

Those organisms have to switch their diet from molecules in the water to ones in each other. Predation. Again, logic. I mean, where have all those tasty molecules gone? *Into* everybody. So what do you eat if you like living? Anybody you can!

Look at the world. Septendecillions of organisms eating other organisms or their products or remnants. A living landscape and sea-scape consuming itself non-stop.

One competitive strategy really gave evolution a shot in the arm: aggregation. Living cells somehow sticking together to form multi-cellular organisms. Result? Us. Us complicated multicellular fungi, plants and animals.

And then there's a variation on aggregation: cooperation. Organisms acting together without integrating into one organism. Organisms—humans included—cooperate as a way of competing. They cooperate to secure nutrition and they cooperate to avoid being somebody else's nutrition.

Man inherited cooperation from eons of predecessors and ran like Roadrunner with it. Humans tend to venerate cooperation, to tremble at the lip when they see it, or think they see it, in the wild: cooperation is good, competition bad. Bear in mind the uniquely human scale of cooperation required in the uniquely human enterprises of environmental despoliation, war and genocide.

Logic. Logical progression. I'm convinced that logical progression accounts for everything that occurs in the universe. I've offered a guess at the logic that dictates some of the key steps in the evolution of life. The rest of this part of the essay argues that nuclear war and environmental despoliation are inescapable steps in this logical progression. Septendecillions of what-can-must logical steps, one triggering the next, have led to the possibility—and thus the inevitability—of both. Nuclear war and environmental despoliation can happen, therefore they must happen. Keep in mind, they already *have* happened. Human ravagement of the environment has been accelerating for centuries, and we've had a nuclear war, a war in which nuclear weapons were used.

We tend to perceive nuclear war and ecological ravage as some kind of deviation from the natural course of things, a deviation for which we humans are responsible and should abominate ourselves. This perception, I believe, blinds us to the true logical origins of these two phenomena and thereby obscures action that will put both safely and permanently behind us.

Man can't be blamed for trashing the environment or contriving superbombs. That's my claim. But if you can't blame him, you can't celebrate him for his stupendous achievements, can you? I can. I celebrate everything. The existence of the universe, the logic that made it the way it is, the logic that made life and made it what *it* is. And I celebrate humanity and all we've accomplished, even if it was logically inevitable we'd accomplish it. Let's look now at how the logic that made it all so worthy of celebration can wreck so much of it.

TECHNOLOGY

Know what I think would be a neat game? People who want to play it do all the studying they want, make all the intellectual, practical and emotional preparation they can think of, then they go to some place they've chosen and start living. They go with nothing. No clothes, no tools, nothing man-made, nothing, for example, that can help them make fire. And they don't get to steal man-made things or use man-made things they find, including primitive technology. They couldn't use an arrowhead, for example, if they found one. They couldn't steal cultivated food, couldn't use a cultivated cotton plant if they ran across one. They'd have to find the stuff in the wild and cultivate it themselves if they wanted to. They couldn't steal domesticated animals. Any animals they domesticate must be wild to begin with.

Advanced preparation could include anything. Players could explore the territory they planned to live in. They could prepare their bodies and skills, e.g. toughen up their feet and practice making fire from either natural materials or with tools they made from natural materials. And they could practice getting food and sleeping outdoors with nothing on. It might be a few days before the players had any shelter (think about building a lean-to without tools). And it would certainly be a while before they had anything like clothing.

Other people could watch (yay, naked people!), photograph, TV news crews could follow the game. No problem. Players and observers could talk to each other all they want, exchange information, observers could even coach the players, provide emotional support, *psychoanalyze* them if they want. But they couldn't supply anything, even natural things, brought, for instance, from another location.

A medical/rescue team could rescue players from danger, injury or sickness. From each other, possibly. Anyone rescued would be removed from the game. They're "dead." Players could have babies. If they were afraid for a baby, the baby could be taken out of the game. Very likely one or both parents would want out too. But if they leave, they can't come back. I'd like to see players have children and raise them in the game. For this, you'd need fertile players of both sexes. In other words, without women the group of players would become extinct. So if all the women *or* men in the game "die," the game is over. One-zip, Environment.

The players would take into the game one "tool," language. Conceivably you could select players who didn't speak the same language, making conditions more like those of our pre-technology forebears who presumably did not communicate verbally. I'd like to save this no-language feature for the super advanced format. I want to see how well the players would do taking into the game all the intangibles they can: language, and plenty of knowledge, training and collaborative preparation. I think it would take as long to prepare players for the game as it took to prepare astronauts for the moon.

Man is technological. You have to go back several species and several millions of years before you can find humanoid ancestors who survived with as little technology as other species use. I use "tools" and "technology" interchangeably to mean inanimate things organisms use to cope with their environment. Things to get food, for example, or to protect themselves from the conditions of their environment or from other organisms. By this definition, a bird's nest—like a human house—is a tool.

Tools are not a human exclusive. Non-humans not only use things they find to perform tasks, they change the things they use. They *make* their tools. Birds make nests. So do lots of animals. Chimpanzees like to remove the leaves from a length of twig and slide it down into termites' nests, pull it out and eat the termites that (foolishly) cling to it. The chimp doesn't simply use the twig as he finds it. He fashions it the way he wants it. He *makes* his tool.

The only difference between man and animals on tools is man makes tools *more*. Much more. He makes tools that make other tools. Tools that make tools that make tools and on and on and on. Of course, man helps the tools make each other, though he may not always in the future.

Technology literally defines man. It's been a major determinant of his physical shape and the genes that dictate it. Tools possibly made our ape-man forebears walk on two feet. Bipedalism this is called, and it distinguishes us from gorillas, chimps and our other closest cousins who usually walk on all four.

Admittedly the oldest tools we've found are about 2.5 million years old, while bipedal australopithecines, our ancestors, go back another 2.5 million years beyond that. But those 2.5 million-year-old tools are recognizable as tools only because australopithecines changed them in some way, like put a crude edge on a rock by banging another rock against it. Certainly australopithecines used rocks long before they started putting edges on them or otherwise permanently marking them, for just throwing or hitting, for example. But those unmarked rocks wouldn't be identifiable today as tools. Yet tools they might have been—five million, maybe more, years ago.

It seems possible to me that our ancestors that walked around on all fours might have thrown rocks at predators to scare them away. Or bopped them with a stick or bone. And the ones who stood straighter could throw further and harder and bop with greater force. And maybe at some point you start throwing and bopping to get dinner for *you*. *You're* the predator. And the straighter you stand, the better you are at throwing and bopping while chasing dinner. Tool use—technology—stands man on his two feet. A possibility.

It's more certain that tools played a role in man's brain growth. Australopithecines' brains were about a quarter the size of ours. The bigger the brain, the more early man was able to do with tools. And the more he did with tools, the more he survived and proliferated. Ergo, brains got bigger and tool use was at least one reason why. Likely the only reason.

The thing I want to see in the game is whether the players—with all their accumulated knowledge from all kinds of fields, with all their planning and rehearsed skills, with all their high-intensity lust for adventure—can "survive." Who knows? Maybe some hot young players could go to the right place and eat and stay warm and alive indefinitely with nothing, including fire. Would I be impressed. No primitive people do it. No *Homo sapiens* ever has.

Another thing I want to see in the game is the sequence in which the players develop their technology. I think it would be the same as it was in history. Again, logic. You need one tool to make the next. To make a hammer you need a stone you can hold in your hand that's well shaped for cutting—like an Acheulian hand ax which goes back a few hundred thousand years. You need it to cut and trim a nice branch for the handle and to open an animal and cut light, good-gripping tendons for tying hammer head to handle. And to make an Acheulian hand ax, you need another stone with at least a crudely sharpened edge, something like the much older Oldowan chopper.

Urgency will also determine the sequential progression of technology in the game. No good starting out planting seeds you've found for vegetables you can eat in a couple of months. You need the time and energy to find food to survive the next 48 hours. Agriculture will have to wait its turn, as it did in history. When fire will appear is anybody's guess. It should be. It's anybody's guess when man first used it. It probably always will be, though the way the game actually plays out could shed some hypothetical light on that.

It seems possible to me that losers developed human technology. Organisms are constantly squeezing members of their own species out of their common econiche. ('Econiche' is my abbreviation of 'ecological niche,' the peculiar set of environmental conditions that enables a kind of organism, a species, to survive.) Organisms have to squeeze fellow species-members out of their common econiche: in order for a species to survive, it has to reproduce more than there's room for. Its members have to produce enough offspring to survive as a species while predators eat them. If they don't, they decline and likely become extinct.

And inside a species, individual members compete over which are going to get squeezed out of the econiche. By definition, an organism can't survive outside its econiche. If it can survive, it's not outside. Outside their econiches, losers don't usually starve or die of exposure. Predators don't give them the opportunity.

Early ancestors of ours must have been squeezed out of their econiche where they too, on their way to starvation or exposure, were eaten by predators. Big predators like lions or little ones like viruses and bacteria. But maybe a squeezed-out individual developed some slight advance in technology that enabled him to survive. Maybe he or she picked up a rock and threw it at a lion and scared it away. Not that this eliminates lions as a threat forever. But it might be a start in systematically reducing the threat. And the more the threat is reduced, the more available a given location is for human habitation. Squeezed-out loser develops technological innovation *and* thereby enlarges the human econiche.

Maybe losers introduce technology, maybe not. But there's no question in my mind that technology enlarges econiches. I think most—conceivably all—of the technological advances man has made have enabled him to live at least a little more in conditions that were previously alien to him. Every technological advance has enlarged his econiche.

The development by our predecessor species *Homo erectus* of improved stone tools and technology to keep warm—fire, primitive clothing—coincides with his spread from southern and eastern Africa to other parts of the world. As early as 1.7 million years ago he appeared in India and Southeast Asia, and a million years later he was in northern China and Europe. These more northerly areas were not open to him prior to his use of animal skins and fire.

Larger econiche means larger population, and *Homo sapiens'* technology explosion has certainly coincided with a population explosion. We *Homo sapiens* originated some 300,000 to 400,000 years ago. There were maybe 10 million of us by 8,000 BC just before the agricultural revolution. That's when we first started cultivating plants and domesticating animals. For millions of years before that we gathered wild plant food and hunted animals to eat. By the year 0 our population had jumped to 300 million.

As a result of the agricultural revolution, humans needed less room to survive. Did we *take* less room? Hell no. Who would? We made more people. 30 times as many in 8,000 years. The agricultural revolution enabled us to expand our econiche not necessarily by spreading out farther into geographical areas we hadn't previously lived in. We expanded our econiche by using much more of the space—including the soil—that we already occupied. In areas where we used to hunt and gather, we cleared away stuff we couldn't eat much of and replaced it with stuff we could. As a result, much larger volumes of the space above the Earth's surface and of the soil beneath it became part of a food chain that fed us.

Human econiche expansion is unique and technology is the reason why. The size of a species' econiche is determined by the structure of the species and the amount of environment in which that structure can survive. Both change, but usually not very fast. The smaller an organism is, the faster its structure can change. There's less to change. And any change is a big one. For big organisms, organisms visible to the naked human eye for example, significant change in structure takes hundreds of thousands or millions of years.

But man has been changing his structure with mounting speed. By changing his technology. I think technology can be viewed as part of physical biological structure. With the wings of an airplane or booster of a rocket, a person can fly. The hammer, in effect, becomes part of our structure when we pick it up and swing it. When we're good at operating it or any technology, we operate it as if it *were* part of our body, without thinking about it. The nice thing about technology is we can disengage it. We can put the hammer down and get out of the rocket. The prosthetic god, Freud calls us.

Technology must be advancing in other species. The abilities to build birds' nests and dip for termites with twigs are not eternal. They started and developed somewhere in history. And if there was progress then, there must be progress now. The only difference between man and other technological species is that his technological progress is faster. Much. And his econiche has been expanding with his technology, both at accelerating rates. The faster they expand, the faster they expand: ten million of us in 8,000 BC, 300 million in 0, one billion in 1850, two billion in 1925 and more than seven billion today. Plot that if you want to see an acceleration curve.

And every enlargement of our econiche diminishes the econiche of other species. We've diminished more than a few econiches to nothing, as we all know. When man develops technology that enables him to keep warm where he used to get too cold, there's less room for species that were there before he moved in. He eats food in his new habitat that other things would have eaten.

Ponder for a moment what an agricultural revolution replaces: all the vegetation that's cleared, that's slashed and burnt away, or uprooted to make room for human crops, all the micro-organisms, insects, birds and other animals that used to eat that removed vegetation, and then all the micro-organisms, insects, birds and other animals that ate *them*, and so on. That whole food chain system that formerly fed man very little is converted to one that feeds him a lot. And it feeds other species that much less, the more so since what man plants he wants all to himself. Much of the history of agriculture, with everything from chicken wire and scarecrows to chemical herbicides and pesticides, is the development of ways to keep micro-organisms, plants, insects, birds and other animals from sharing the soil, crops and animals that man is cultivating.

Today most non-human econiches are diminishing as a result of the accelerating expansion of man's econiche. Many species have disappeared. Others are on their way. The only exceptions are domesticated animals, cockroaches, viruses—human pets and pests. Things that feed off us. These guys' econiches are expanding with ours.

I believe several things occur at the climax of any life system. Every life system sooner or later produces a "technological" species, a species that develops the complex of technology that we've developed. And this species inevitably dominates the life system. At the climax, this dominant species completes—or threatens to complete—the transformation of the entire life system into one that feeds that species with optimal efficiency. Species that don't contribute to the food chain that feeds the dominant species tend to disappear.

So what? So the monkeys, giraffes, elephants and so on disappear because we barbed-wire them out and raise wheat or cattle there instead. I imagine that wiping out all species that aren't required in a man-feeding food chain presents no threat to man's indefinite survival. We might have to increase *our* physical contribution to such a system. We'd have to stop sealing dead people up in containers that other organisms can't get into. And make sure our sewage gets to the microorganisms at the bottom of the chain. The circle has to be complete.

I think of this outcome of a life system's story as the "Soylent Green" scenario. You may know of this movie from some years back, Charlton Heston and Edward G. Robinson. In it, the world is packed full of people who've eaten up everything and are left with only state-supplied Soylent Green cakes. Heston at the end discovers Soylent Green to be processed people who, like Robinson, have been voluntarily—but with much encouragement—terminated.

I've changed "Soylent Green" to mean, not a system where people eat only other people, but a tightly restricted food chain cycle whose exclusive purpose is to feed one species, the dominant, technological species, in our case people.

One image from the movie is particularly applicable to the Soylent Green scenario proposed here. Robinson is put away surrounded by pastoral music and movies of deer, rabbits and other wildlife frolicking in meadows and forests. Of course, all this wildlife—including the meadows and forests—no longer exists. A life system with just us, what we eat and what we eat eats and so on around the circle would probably work fine. It must be what scientists planning colonies in space have in mind. The only damage would be esthetic. And psychological. I'd be wrecked. I don't want it, even long after *I've* terminated.

Sounds like another polemic against man's ravagement of the environment, doesn't it? It isn't. I'm glad what's happened happened. Not specifically the ravagement, though that's an inescapable part of what I'm glad about. The agricultural revolution, the industrial revolution, the chemical, the computer, even the nuclear revolution. All the technological revolutions that have resulted in the explosive growth of man's econiche and with it man's population. It could happen, it had to happen. Some other species would have done it if we hadn't, sooner or later. Some species will do it sooner or later in any life system. In any universe, I think.

Good might come of it all. Consummate good. It might not. But it might. The possibility is what I'm glad about, and what this essay is about.

CONSUMPTION

Soylent Green climaxes man's competition with other species, nuclear war climaxes his competition with other humans. These two occur at the climax of any life system, I believe. The logic of the way life works directs evolution at them. Here's how.

Life is growth. Even if a species' econiche is all filled up, even if a whole life system's econiche is all filled up and there's no room for growth, still the essential characteristic of life there—or anywhere—is growth.

All organisms grow, at least for a while. And after they've grown a while, some replicate. More growth. Inevitably all this growth has to bump into itself. The stuff the organisms need to eat in order to grow and replicate has to run out. The logically unavoidable result of growth is competition.

Species of organisms have to grow fast enough to survive being eaten by predators. A stupefying picture, to me: millions of species eating each other and, at the same time, reproducing fast enough to keep all the species remarkably close to the same size over long periods of time. And essential to this marvelous balance is the drive in all species to grow.

Feelings drive growth. Hunger communicates to the organism's consciousness the organism's need for food, which it needs to grow. Things like plants may not get hungry, but their constituent cells do, I bet.

And in species that reproduce sexually, the feeling of lust, of sexual need, communicates to the organism's consciousness the species' need for reproduction, which the species needs to grow. It's a little different with plants that reproduce sexually, but organisms that move around freely have to feel lust. Something has to attract them to other organisms for making offspring and contributing to their species' growth. Who cares about making offspring and contributing to species growth? Nobody. Who wants to satisfy lust? Everybody.

But what does all this growth-need have to do with humans? Do we, as a species, have to grow? Our only predators are microscopic, and they're not threatening us with extinction. The only species doing that is us, and nobody I know of is claiming more growth will help there.

So the logic behind the growth drive in other species is missing in our own. Why then are we humans growing? If we didn't try to grow, maybe we wouldn't compete so much with each other and with nonhuman organisms. Less competition with nonhumans—less growing into econiches they occupy—then less ecological ravage. Maybe no ravage, no *new* ravage. Maybe even human retrenchment someday, give other species *back* some space. And less competition with other humans, less war, maybe no war. No nuclear war. No *more* nuclear war.

What do we mean by human growth? First, we have to mean population growth. We all know the world's human population is exploding, and we all know why. Technology. Accelerating improvements in food production and medical care. Death rates are declining at all age levels and birth rates don't always decline with death rates.

Ecologists report that exploding populations in developing countries are replacing about two percent of the world's jungles each year with agriculture. Though most of the Earth's oxygen is supplied by photosynthesis in the oceans, conversion of the jungles to agriculture would radically diminish a significant oxygen source. Pretty cheeky of us affluents to complain, though, after we got ours. Much of the northern hemisphere was forest as little as a thousand years ago. It's not now. Why not let *our* forests come back before putting the heat on poor folks for cutting theirs? Let your entirely decorative front lawn go back to forest before bitching about what others are doing to survive.

Also, the question few want to ask is how much the various forms of subsidies from affluent countries have stimulated third world population growth and, thereby, jungle depletion. Rock and a hard place: let them starve, or help them help us trash the joint.

Population growth is only one part of human growth. The world's human population could be standing still, *declining*, and we'd still be savaging the place. Growth also has to mean growth in consumption, growth of our take from the environment, our take from other organisms. All growth is at someone or something else's expense.

It's not headline news that human consumption is growing, or that most of this growth is in the world's rich, hi-tech countries. The average American consumes 40 times as much as the average inhabitant of India. India's population would have to be growing 40 times as fast as ours to match our consumption. Think about *that* when planning your next wee one, your next piranha. Makes our suggestions regarding third world population growth sound, again, pretty cheeky, don't you think? Maybe the third world has some suggestions for us on how to consume less. (Not likely, of course. Third world people have every intention of consuming the way we do as soon as they can. Those that already can do.)

Why do we affluents consume so much? Why is our rate of consumption growing so fast? Consumption's a funny thing. In the case of much of what modern affluent humans uniquely consume, it isn't the taking of the stuff that costs other organisms. It's what we do with it. Much of what we affluents consume is made from stuff dug up from the Earth, from below the biosphere, the layer of the Earth's surface where organisms live. We don't take anything from other organisms by pulling up minerals, coal, oil and natural gas. What we do with it, though, costs all organisms, us included.

Hauling massive volumes of stuff up from underground and spreading it all over the surface of the Earth in the form of housing, offices, factories, storage facilities, military installations, airports, highways, railroads, parking lots and pavements, all this eliminates life. Add to this the hard mantle that man is laying over the Earth the fields, pastures and feed lots that grow food just for us, and add to them all golf courses, sports fields, ski slopes, manicured parks and suburban lawns—America's suburban lawns could form a major country—and you have a picture of the life system affluent man is snuffing out or converting to food chains whose single purpose is to feed and entertain us. This covered and converted surface and the energy that flows within it, generated mostly by fossil fuels whose exhausts further assault living things, is the sum and substance of the affluent world's good life, the growth with a capital G that is today's virtually unchallenged definition of economic health.

Why are we doing it? What drives you and me to do it? And let's get that straight. It *is* you and me. It's not *them*. It's you and I that work in the offices and factories, buy their products, get *and want* the military protection—I mean if you don't want it, there are plenty of places where it's not to be had; and it's no coincidence you won't find the life you're used to there. It's you and I that ride the highways and railroads, live in the housing, park in the parking lots, walk on the pavements and spew up landmasses of garbage while we're doing it. Unless you're out in the woods playing The Game, you're participating in all this. I am.

What drives us to consume all this stuff? The answer couldn't be simpler or more obvious. We want it. The frightening thing is that so much of what we want is so entirely logical to want, so hard, so dumb, so self-destructive not to grab the minute it becomes available and the minute we can afford it.

I have two key points to make in this essay. Here's the first. The logic that drives affluent humanity's ravenously destructive consumption today is precisely the same logic that drives all organisms at all stages of development everywhere to do whatever they do. We consume all the stuff we do for the same reasons all organisms anytime anywhere do anything.

All organisms will do anything to avoid death whenever and however it threatens. It's the nature of organisms: we want to live forever. Exceptions are rare.

To stay alive, all organisms need to eat, most if not all need to rest, some need to avoid things that threaten death, and some individuals of all species must reproduce for the species to survive. Organisms are driven by feelings associated with these needs. Without the feelings, the organisms and their species wouldn't meet the needs and therefore wouldn't survive.

But not all these needs apply to all organisms, so the feelings probably don't apply either. It'd be sort of mean, for instance, if plants could feel fear, the emotion that tells an organism to avoid danger. I mean, what could a plant do about what it's afraid of?

Eat, rest, avoid danger and reproduce. Most, maybe all, the body functions and activities of organisms serve to accomplish these tasks. And what do all these boil down to but safety? Safety from death. Eat and you're safe from starvation or from diminished energy that makes you an easier target for predators. Rest and you're safe from, again, diminished energy. Avoid dangers, like predators that threaten you no matter how much energy you've got. Avoid dangers like falling, or banging into something. Reproduce—by having sex, if that's how your species works. Reproduce and your species is safe from extinction. Safer.

What about humans? Humans are organisms. Do all our grand enterprises and achievements, our Hamlets and Sistine Chapels, our I Am The Emperors, boil down to these menial essentials? Eating? Sleeping? Avoiding danger? Well, it certainly isn't reproducing: little human sex activity has anything to do with *that* anymore. Eat, sleep, avoid danger, have sex? That's it?

It's a lot of it, I think. Human consumption equals human safety. Much—if not all—of what humans consume provides safety from death that we wouldn't have if we didn't consume it. Weapons are consumption. And weapons have always provided humans safety they wouldn't have had without them, first from predators and later from hunger. After humans figured out how to use the sticks and stones they scared predators away with to hunt, they became dependent on their weapons for food. Dependent because hunting enabled their numbers to grow beyond what earlier feeding methods alone could support.

And if other humans want the territory where you're gathering and hunting food—because *they* need the food that can be gathered and hunted there—then your weapons and skills with them are critical to your safety. From either death in battle or, again, hunger, caused by your being driven out of the food-providing territory.

In fact, you're irresponsible not to use your weapons and weapons skills to drive other humans out of a territory that can feed you, your offspring and those with whom you're interdependent. Not to do so would be arbitrarily to limit your own growth, development and longevity and that of those closest to you, your children for instance. A form of self-sacrifice that might not be reciprocated. Using weapons to expand your territory, to take food sources from other organisms, including other humans, increases the safety of you and yours from death. The logic of life is not lions lying down with lambs.

The agricultural revolution and the spectacular increases in human consumption that came with it spectacularly increased human safety. The agricultural revolution enabled some 30 times as many people to live. Again, more food in the world for humans, more humans—at all age levels—living longer. They're 30 times safer than they were before from hunger and death.

The Industrial Revolution. What was safe about that? Overcrowded cities, lousy sanitation, dangerous factories, young children working in them, pollution of everything, lousy wages, lousy physical and emotional health, lousy lousy lousy. In retrospect.

But at the time, conditions had to look like an improvement, for workers as well as capitalists, or the Industrial Revolution wouldn't have happened. It offered people something when the only alternative was nothing. If conditions were better on the farm, the workers would have stayed there. The population of Britain, where the Revolution first ignited, tripled between 1750 and 1850. The ability of Britain's economy to support human life tripled during those years of industrial Big Bang. This is added safety for people who simply wouldn't have been alive had the Industrial Revolution not happened. Safety through increased consumption—in which everyone participates to some degree.

How much of our consumption today affords us affluents safety we wouldn't have if we didn't consume it? We'd die earlier without much of the medical care we consume. Safety's a big reason for living and working in the kinds of buildings we do. Most of what we do to food is in the interests of safety. The chemical fertilizers, pesticides and animal growth promotants we use in our food production might give some of us cancer. But for the moment at least, the bottom line on these agents is much more food than there would be without them, and thus increased safety from starvation. With a car, it's easier to live where people and all the things you need to get to—work, bank, stores—are spread out. And whatever they say, it's still safer where people are spread out—suburbia—than in the pack-and-stack people warehouses downtown.

But is a top-of-the-line Porsche with customized engine and body for say $180,000 really 19 times safer than an old brown Corolla, $9,500 new? And do we really need all the house most of us live in to be really safe? People all over the world cram by the scads into dwellings the size of the family room. (I'm talking village cozy here, not pack-and-stack urban.) And do we really confine our medicines to ones that stand between us and death? Hah!

Safety plays its part. But at this point it looks like there's a lot more to affluent human consumption than just safety.

Try this slant.

In the wild, biological features spread evenly throughout a species. Each individual is biologically about as well-adapted to the environment as a member of that species can be. If it's not, it doesn't survive. If it's a lot better, it produces offspring that, over generations, take over the species. Age differences, sex differences, one guy's horns a little longer than another's, okay. But generally speaking, species members in the wild are pretty much the same. As a result, inside most species it's socially flat, comparatively. There's hierarchy, pecking order. But there's nothing like the prodigious socio-economic differences found among civilized humans.

Unlike biological features, technology doesn't spread evenly among members of the species that's making and using the technology—at least not initially. Some individuals get the skills to make or use a piece of technology before others do, giving them more power than the others. These individuals compete with each other for the same reasons all organisms compete. So if a technological skill means a competitive advantage, who wants to share it? Share it when it serves your own interests, with people you're cooperating with, but not with competitors. (And don't go hog wild with people you're cooperating with.)

Technology tends to accrete, to accumulate where other technology already exists. Individuals who are most skilled in making or using a hand-ax, a potter's wheel, a computer are most likely to be the ones to discover improvements, to advance the technology, and thereby acquire a *greater* competitive advantage.

The result: individuals in technological cultures get on top of each other and groups of others and on top of groups of groups. Social pyramids. Pyramids of pyramids. Just add technology and people form them like crystals. Competition plus technology equals hierarchy.

Today's Fortune 500 corporation chairman needs few hands-on technology skills to do his job. Nevertheless, it's technology that gives him his power. He controls the people who control the technology. If the corporation works right, the chairman has the best general and integrated grasp of all the technologies that drive the corporation: production, new product research and development, marketing, law. (I think of most law as abstraction of technology. Most law is about things, mostly man-made things—technology—and about people's relationship to the things and to each other regarding the things.)

Inevitably, the chairman built his power on mastery of one of these individual technologies.

What about a rock star? What's how far he gets up the hierarchy got to do with technology? People put technology around him when he performs. They figure the investment in a stadium concert or album will make money. They don't put the technology around the rock star's backers or the technicians or you or me. The rock star's got technological power that his backers, technicians, you and I don't have. It's not the man who makes the sword who has the power. It's the man who wields it. Ever notice? Same with paper, pen and ink. And microphone.

Technological species are hierarchical species. At least for a while they are. We humans are still living in that while.

Individuals compete for places in the hierarchies that technology creates. We humans certainly do. Humans survive by being parts of human cultures. I can't think of an exception. Holy men of India take alms. They're not out hunting and gathering food on their own. They're not playing the super-*super* advanced format of The Game. Solo. Nobody is.

And to be part of human culture is to have a place in some human hierarchy. And to have a place is to have something that somebody else wants. And to want something somebody else has. Why? Why do we want to go up the hierarchy we're in? Why can't we be satisfied with where we are? Because the higher we go, the easier it is to get the things we want and need. And since much—maybe all—of what we want and need relates to safety, it's safer the further up the hierarchy you go. And more safety is what all sane organisms want.

How do you get up the hierarchy? You need two things, I think. You need superior skill in making, using and/or controlling technology. And you need superior skill in interacting with other people. You need allies, people to help you, you need to be able to get things from people, to be good at influencing, even dominating and controlling other people, at keeping them from challenging you. You need to be able to hold on to competitive advantages you've won, to keep people in their own damned place. Social oppression? Sometimes. It's what competition in a technological species can become.

In hierarchy competition, identity is vital. Strong, brave, rich, smart, sexy, wise, simple, kind, ancient and august pedigree. Who are you? What are you? You need to let people know. And without having to prove it all the time. You need to wear it, drive it, live in it, decorate your office with it. You need to talk it, but not directly. You tell people how tough you are by putting "fuckin'" between all words. That tells 'em. If you're smart, say "chthonic" or "transude" a lot. Old money, say "fun and attractive." Gay: "Love your outfit."

And you need to do all this identifying inside the subtle and treacherous identity games that always grow up in all hierarchies and that are always changing. Never over-identify, for example. Be careful about driving Rolls-Royces. Don't wear I Am The Emperor on your blazer (great T-shirt idea though). Don't be too pretentious. At least not on the East Coast. In L.A. be totally pretentious or you'll drown.

Identity works two ways. On the one hand you want your identity to have some favorable impact on others. On the other, *you* want to know who's worth knowing, dealing with, who'd be a good ally, who'd be good for support, pushes and pulls up the hierarchy, who's worth the effort of impacting. You need to know *their* identities.

How do we identify ourselves? Lots of ways. The way we move, the way we walk and talk, the words we use, the things we talk about, our "accents," which we consciously form. I think our Southern, our patrician, our blue-collar tough accents don't form spontaneously.

But the identity-forming and -presenting activity I'm interested in is consuming. That's what we're talking about here: human consumption.

Everything we affluents consume has a practical purpose: feed us, keep us warm, dry, safe, lift our spirits, cleanse our souls, stuff like that. But most of what we consume to accomplish all this has a secondary purpose, often representing *most* of the cost. Identity. Identity consumption. The $180,000 Porsche, whether or not it got us up the hierarchy, is a mobile reminder that up the hierarchy is where we're at. That's a lot of why we put that kind of money into a car. It makes us important to other people and gives us enormous power we simply don't have without it.

The clothes we wear, the neighborhoods we live in, how we interior decorate, what we drive, read, just about everything all of us spend money on identifies us. Are we rich, smart, tough, athletic, old-fashioned, aristocratic, religious, hip, dangerous, cynical, sexy, sexual, do we have no time for all this silly identity crap, and on and on and on. The message is in the precise selections of what we buy and display.

We identity consume to win acceptance from other people. If we're not accepted, we don't, for instance, get laid. Definitive acceptance, wouldn't you say? And is there any argument whether we identity consume to get it? That about 99 percent of $180,000 Porsche equals sex? In the affluent segments of today's world, sexual feelings stimulate consumption growth, not population growth. Interesting, isn't it?

Being accepted is getting laid, having friends, family, being interdependent with others so you can make money and otherwise survive and prosper. Being accepted is serious business. Don't get accepted and we fall in the hierarchy. Fall in the hierarchy and we find ourselves in an alien environment: closer to the bottom towards which people progressively play rougher to stay in the game. Where they've spent their lives playing rougher, where they're experienced at it. Where we haven't and aren't. Falling in the hierarchy is dangerous. And identity consumption is one way we protect ourselves from doing it.

The definitive barometer of acceptance and rejection is feelings. It feels great when you're being accepted and lllousy when you're not. And feeling lousy counts. It puts you closer to death. People kill themselves when they feel lousy. Or they do lousy on the job, jeopardizing job. Lose their job and they *might* kill themselves. If they don't get another job, they might starve. More realistically, they might take things to stop feeling lousy. Things that might shorten their lives. Feeling lousy is life-threatening.

Human consumption equals human safety. Safety from falling in the hierarchy and safety from feeling bad about it. Both of which are dangerous. Strong motives to identity consume, I think. That's the slant. An enormous segment of affluent human consumption is identity consumption. And no matter how tacky and bourgeois it may seem, if identity consumption provides safety that can't be had without it, then you're dumb not to play. Which is why we all do.

Other things drive humans to consume. Humans suppress their feelings. Maybe they always have. Maybe lots of species do. Maybe being a multicellular organism requires constituent cells to suppress feelings to function in a way that beats going it alone.

Humans, I'm convinced, suppressed their feelings increasingly as their technology developed. It makes sense. They needed to cooperate more and with increasing precision to get the most out of their advancing technology. Acting out a lot of wild feelings would get in the way and disrupt that increasingly precise cooperation.

I've often wondered whether we *had* to suppress our feelings, whether technology and civilization might have progressed just as well, or better, were people free to experience their fear, anger, pain, etc. Not act them out necessarily. Just feel them, completely. It's the great organizer, warfare, that suggests not. As warfare developed and increasingly required precisely integrated human action to optimize the effectiveness of advancing military technology, there was less room for, shall we say, emotional diversity. And successful social behavior in battle—suppressing feelings of terror, for instance—becomes the model for behavior in all situations. Reasonable. What worked in the crunch should work the rest of the time, wouldn't you think?

Either way, there's not a shred of doubt in my mind that all affluent humans suppress their feelings. We don't feel them. Not anywhere near fully. We try to control them, to feel good all the time. And we consume all kinds of things—books, seminars, retreats and the like along with the powders and potions—to do it.

We affluents are addictive consumers. We consume all kinds of things to feel better. New dress, car stereo, I'll feel better if I buy one. Origin of all addictions, right? Stop feeling bad?

Key Point Number One claims that we humans consume all the stuff we do for the same reasons all organisms anytime anywhere do anything. So how is consumption aimed at controlling feelings comparable to what nonhuman organisms do? I think safety's involved. Safety from what? From social rejection. Expressing or acting on feelings alienates people and thereby weakens the individual's ties to the social fabric. Come loose from the social fabric and you either die or other people support you. They do *your* surviving. And they don't reward you with a lot of respect for the privilege.

Suppress those feelings and you won't express them or act on them. Suppress the rage that they moved the pet care section again. *Don't* scream uncontrollably, foam at the mouth, roll around in the aisle and pull down stacks of canned soup and corn flakes. Suppress that fatigue, the fear the job's too big for you. Suppress the depression. Ever notice the first thing they show you on a new job is where the coffee's made?

Bite a Marlboro from the box, cowboy, when you're feeling like a grov-eling drip. Loosen up at the party or it might be your last.

You're stupid if you don't want what coffee, cigarettes, booze and drugs give you. Productive, self-confident, turned-on and fun not only feel good, they mean surviving, making a place for yourself in the hierarchy, friends, being needed. Not is not. And not is danger-ous. Life-threateningly. That's why people go at these mood-alterers like sharks in a blood frenzy. They're not stupid. Well, they *wouldn't* be if the agents themselves weren't life-threatening. And how much can a little hurt? Most people are barely scratched by immoderate use of the various mood-alterers. Either way, mood-alterers are a big part of our economy, of affluent human consumption. And I think, like most consumption, it's consumption for safety, ultimately from death.

Two major forces behind affluent human consumption: the need for identity and the need to control feelings. There are others. Pleasure. Fun. They drive our consumption. Not that that makes our motives any different from those of other organisms. It's my guess that eating, resting, and successfully avoiding danger are fun for anything that does them. Surviving as a species, at least for those who do it sexually, is fun. Hell, if it's how you propagate, maybe splitting in two's a gas, the ultimate orgasm.

The things organisms do to survive individually and as a species are fun (when they do them successfully). I'd argue that all pleasure that organisms in the wild experience relates to survival and safety. Cuddling's fun. But a lot of the pleasure is in feeling safe. In *being* safe. Among those species that do it, cuddling is part of rest, warmth, pro-tection from predators. And fatigue, cold and being eaten are certainly unsafe, and presumably unfun.

Aren't baby mammals intoxicating when they fight each oth-er? Biting, grunting, climbing all over and swallowing each other?

Killing's fun. The thrill a lion experiences bringing down an antelope must consume its entire body and consciousness. And obviously, for carnivorous mammals—the ones whose young are so cute when they fight—it's unsafe not to kill.

We affluents have fun. Music, movies, travel. But I think the fun we have can be related to safety. A lot of identifying, for example, going on in our fun. Safety-oriented identifying. I'm this kind of person because I like *this* kind of music, liked *that* movie. Touch me, I *went* there. Backpacked. I'm a backpacker. The drive here is for social safety, for a strong bond in the social fabric, strong position in the hierarchy, lookin' good. Social safety that consuming, to a large extent, buys.

Sex is fun, right? A lot of identifying going on though, any argument there? I don't mean just leading up to, I mean right *in* it. Do I do this now? Am I *natural* enough? No way she can tell what I'm *really* fantasizing, IS THERE? Identity stuff. *Safety* stuff. Social safety, emotional safety. Safety that in affluent culture involves consumption. Of, for instance, endless magazines and self-help books telling you what you're supposed to do when and how, and how important it is to be "natural."

People aren't stupid. They do what they need to do. They get to a certain stage of cultural development, a stage determined by how far their technology has advanced, and they consume. They consume for the same reasons all organisms do anything. Any organism would. Affluent human consumption is determined by a few of the septendecillions of logical steps that make all things in the universe do what they do. Dangerous and destructive as it is, affluent human consumption isn't some deviation from this logical process. Deviations from this process don't happen, I think. Universes don't work that way.

House, second car, some new clothes (wore this bag to church twice already). Innocent, wholesome, loyal American dreams. What's the harm?

None. The culprit behind accelerating growth of affluent consumption is not the *desire* to consume, the *effort* to get more, all of which translates into the human species' desire and effort to grow. All species desire and try to grow. All organisms do things that make their species *try* to grow. But only humans *get* to grow. Why?

Technology's the culprit. Technology that with increasing speed removes conditions that previously limited humanity's ability to survive. Technology that enables us to keep beating back other species in the competition for nutrition-supplying space. They'd do it to us if they could, wouldn't they?

Size of econiche is determined by structure of the organism and the environment to which the organism adapts. With technology we, in effect, change our physical structure. Faster and faster. If advancing technology doesn't clear the space for human growth, that growth doesn't happen.

I believe that if accelerating human technology suddenly ground to a halt, froze in place and stayed there, the growth of the human econiche would stop. Even at a very high level of technological development. High technology does not expand econiches. Technological *advancement*, at any level, expands them. So if human technology froze in place, so would the human econiche. And with it, human population and consumption.

Which, in a way, is what I think is going to happen. I'm counting on our glorious technology that got us into this mess to get us out. Part 3 argues that technology, as it relates to our daily lives, is nearing saturation. Saturation of *its* econiche. It won't be long before it has essentially done all it can for our lives. We'll be as safe from the environment, predators of all sizes, natural catastrophes, as technology can make us. And that'll be plenty safe enough.

Saturation level technology plus the fill-yourself-up, total self-gratification cultural flip *we* have to make in the way we think and behave—these two will not only stop the growth of the human species and its consumption but enable both to decline. Rapidly, pleasurably and productively. Everybody wins. Hundred million of us or so, using about as much of the Earth as when we were that size before. Doing it for millions of years. Billions maybe. That's the way it'll be because that's the way we'll want it. We didn't get to be master species just to make ourselves miserable. Or, I think, to destroy ourselves.

Nuclear war

Here's a couple of quotes that piss me off: "Ethology, the study of behavior, has yet to find the evolutionary basis of man's aberrant conduct that allows him to kill members of his own species wholesale, which other species do not do."

That's English zoologist Sir Gavin de Beer writing in the Encyclopedia Britannica. Some years ago a writer in the Canadian Journal of Politics and Science wondered "how mankind seemingly alone among animals is capable of killing others of his own species on a massive scale and without compunction."

Don't get me wrong. War's not my idea of a fun way to spend the afternoon. Or one's youth. I've never been involved in one and I'm glad.

It's the put-down in these quotes that I hate. Humans are "aberrant." They kill "without compunction." How does he know they kill without compunction? Does he? These guys may not know why humans fight wars, but they certainly know they're bad for doing it.

I disagree. I don't think we're bad or aberrant for that or anything else. Wars don't happen because people are bad or aberrant. Or because they're stupid and greedy. No organisms are stupid, and they're all greedy. But only humans have wars. Why?

I think two ingredients are key to war: the growth drive, shared by all organisms, and technology that's advanced enough to support agriculture.

Humans, like all species, are driven to grow. And in an environment of limited size—is there any other kind?—growing things compete with each other. You could argue that every living organism in a life system competes, however indirectly, with every other living organism.

Why has competition with other humans driven humans to kill each other in large numbers when killing is rare within other species? Intraspecies competition yes, but why the killing? Why war?

Right off, the question makes humans look bad—unfairly, I think. Wolves are one of many kinds of animals that fight each other ferociously over, among other things, territory but refrain from killing once the adversary cowers in defeat. Some species-preserving instinct that humans don't have is said to come into play. I wonder.

The implication is that spared loser wolf simply wanders off and finds some territory somewhere else. Some other area that can supply his food and that has the other characteristics that enable him to survive. Some other part of the wolf econiche. But wherever that is, who says other wolves aren't there already? And who says loser wolf, weakened by his last battle and the food he *didn't* get as a result—then or since—will have any better luck getting into some other food-supplying territory? Wolf growth would tend to fill up all wolf territories, I'd think, putting loser outside wolf econiche to perish. So it doesn't matter whether winner wolf in the fight-not-to-the-death administers the *coup de grace*. The result's the same. Why waste the energy?

Killing is how life works. Organisms survive only by eating other organisms, or their products or remnants. And organisms compete desperately for the privilege of eating each other. Losers not only don't eat, they're sooner eaten.

To me, there's a mathematical beauty to it all: a spherical mosaic embracing the Earth's surface, a mosaic of species eating other species about as fast as they're being eaten themselves, the molecular constituents of the mosaic moving among all the mosaic tiles, all the species. Powering the whole process is solar energy absorbed by plants and other photosynthesizers. The energy is passed along when the photosynthesizers get eaten. Round round round. Eat eat eat. Right now you're probably made of components that have passed through every imaginable kind of organism since life began.

What's really beautiful is the way the size of the mosaic tiles stay the same for such long periods. That's because the species' drive to grow is perfectly counter-balanced by their predators' eating. If it weren't perfectly balanced, a species would either be destroyed by predators or it would get bigger, more numerous. As numerous as predators and other conditions allowed it to get. *Then* it would be perfectly balanced. Logic.

That's one way of looking at it. But if killing's what you find distasteful about war, take a look at life and the logic that drives it.

I think most of us are still victims of the vision of nature as some kind of peaceable kingdom of plenty. There is plenty, but it's all plenty of each other, because that's who everybody's eating. How bad does war look compared to that? To take a realistic look at nature in the wild is to conclude, I believe, that it's nowhere you want to be. I mean, who's stopping you? Rip off your clothes, jump out there and play The Game. At least wars end. They take a break.

It's no coincidence that the only species that kills others of its species in large numbers is also the only one with well-developed technology. It seems likely to me, for a species to engage in war involving large-scale killing, technology has to be advanced enough to support agriculture. The earliest indications of war—remnants of fortifications and representations of war in art—are associated with agricultural civilizations. Cultures that preceded agriculture and that could have portrayed war in their art, like those that painted the caves in southern France and Spain, didn't. These paintings portray humans killing animals, sometimes on a large scale. But they're not killing humans.

Agriculture involves larger accumulations of food than hunting and gathering do. You don't spend several months raising grain just to eat it all in a couple of meals. You need enough to hold you until you raise some more. Which you may not be able to *start* doing for many months. That's a lot of grain. Enough for a group large enough to maintain the complex of technology necessary to support agriculture. *And* large enough to protect the agriculture/technology complex from theft by outsiders—human or otherwise. There has to be enough grain and other food for all those people for many months, maybe years (seven lean ones, for example).

For anyone who had a bad year, that quantity of food is worth taking some chances for. "Stealing that grain would be wrong, son. We didn't grow it, so it's not ours. We'll just have to starve to death." Legitimacy of ownership just doesn't cut it under all circumstances. You've got to fight over food sometimes. When the alternative is dying, for instance.

But why can't we be like other animals, wolves for instance, and just fight and chase the losers off? Why do we have to kill? Why do we have to get *aberrant* about it? Next thing we'll be killing *without compunction!*

Well, what's to prevent the people you chased away from all that accumulated food from sneaking back at night—nights of any one of the days, months, years it'll take you and yours to eat it all? What's to prevent them from either stealing the food away or attacking you for it when you're off-guard? I think killing them might prevent that, what do you think? And if your technology is advanced enough to grow grain, you've got *great* things for killing people. You've been killing animals for hundreds of thousands of years. And not with your bare hands. Beat those plowshares into nifty swords.

Agriculture concentrates things. It concentrates food. Prior to agriculture, food that feeds all kinds of species is all mixed up with each other. Agriculture replaces that mix-up with food for one species exclusively. Food concentration. Which results in people concentration. More people can survive in one place than had ever been possible before. And for a longer time. By a lot.

Not only does agriculture allow large numbers of people, it requires them. What can must. It takes a lot of technology to support agriculture. Technology to cultivate crops, to move large quantities of them and store them for long periods, metal and pottery vessels for carrying and heating water and for cooking, implements for grinding grain, a principal product of agriculture. Ovens for baking pottery and bread. It takes a lot of people to make and maintain all this technology. You also need people who can make and use military technology, to keep out outsiders who want the food *and* the technology.

This concentration of food and people is explosive. Not only are the agriculturalists concentrated, they're much less mobile than they were as hunter/gatherers. Their skills are geared to agriculture and its supporting technology. When the crop doesn't come up, they can't fall back on earlier methods of survival. They've lost the skills. Even if they haven't, where would all those agriculturalists—that agriculture has enabled *and required* to proliferate—be absorbed? Hunting/gathering can't support those numbers.

So there you are. A whole lot of agriculturalists concentrated together, confined together, in contact with each other on a scale not possible prior to agriculture. And the crop doesn't come up. No food. And technology all around that's so sharp, so wieldable, so adaptable to killing. Any sane organism would use all he's got—things, and skills in using them—to get and keep food for himself and for those dependent on him. A food crisis at this stage of technology is a natural for bloodletting, either within a given agriculture/technology complex or between two or more of them. War. A rarity, I'd think, among more mobile and spread-out hunter/gatherers.

Why have we humans fought and killed each other nonstop through the ages? We've fought to stay alive, to defend ourselves and those we love. We've fought over land, land that produces food for ourselves and for our technology, i.e. metals and other minerals, and coal, oil and natural gas. Technology food.

Without food, people die. So it's understandable that we go to any extreme to secure it. Any organism would. The same applies to raw materials for our technology, our technology food. We become dependent on our latest technological advances, and their loss can be life threatening. Take away the oil that fuels contemporary affluent civilization and you threaten the lives of the civilization and the people in it. At any given stage of technology, there are more people than any earlier stage could have supported. Ergo, regress technologically and you lose people. So if killing protects your technology and your technology food, killing's what you do.

We've also fought and killed over trade arteries across land and water, through which travel things we need and things we trade to get them. Same deal. You adapt to the availability of those goods and markets, and, as a result, their loss is life terminating.

Freedom, justice, honor, revenge. Principles, ideals, slogans. We've fought over them. But I think we've fought more *with* such things than over them. Principles, ideals and slogans justify action to secure land and trade routes. They enhance the motive to fight, for example in cultures where legitimacy of ownership concepts are strong, where guilt might cast a pall over the taking of the needed. And principles, ideals and slogans can embody or be critical components of what makes a culture work the way it does, making it stronger than others, the winner of, among other things, wars.

Yes, liberate the holy places. God wills it. But a Crusade would also put a wedge in the gut of the Muslim growth coming at us from all sides. Spain, North Africa, the Mediterranean: in 1095, when the First Crusade was launched, Europe seemed surrounded by Muslims. The immediate terror was the Seljuq Turks' conquest of Orthodox Christian Asia Minor, threatening Constantinople and, with it, Latin Christianity's eastern flank. An entirely sane terror: whole peoples had ceased to exist during such conquests. More than religious idealism drove the Crusaders.

Yes, slavery's an abomination. Particularly if it's in *all* U.S. territories, which the Dred Scott decision permitted (imagine slavery in Minnesota). Big Southern planters buy up all the land, and, for us little guy Northerners saving up to homestead the west, Manifest Destiny is down the tube. We're fenced out. Exclusive, or at least equitable access to the unsettled territories, the Great Plains and the Wild West—now that's worth fighting for.

Are today's Shiite Moslems fighting their rival Sunnis to make them into Shiites? Make them see the light? No. Shiites are fighting to get what the Sunnis have. Land, influence, better access to economic and political power. Nutrition. More of it and more easily gotten. Jihad holy war fires the Shiites up, pulls them together, legitimizes *their* having it all rather than the Sunnis, Druzes, Christians or Jews. Or other Shiites.

Look to the core of even the most fanatically idealistic conflicts and I think you'll find material grievances, nests of them, constantly being fed by new ones. Frankly, if I believed people left behind adequate food and the safety of home to kill—which I'm convinced repels all people, at least initially—to subject themselves to intense fear and possibly long and excruciating pain and death solely for ideals, principles and slogans, I'd think we *were* aberrant.

War, I'm convinced, is an entirely sane, rational and necessary human enterprise. And I'm convinced we won't escape the need for it until we understand how it works and why it keeps happening, why it's been a permanent fixture in all human life for the last 10,000 years.

I believe that the logic of what life is and the way life works has constantly required humans above a certain level of technology to go to war. Over and over again. Non-stop. And the same kind of logic is driving us to nuclear war now.

We all want more. We want as much as we can get. We want as much as is available, as much as we know about. No, we want as much as we can *imagine*. Any organism would. What are feelings for? They're for surviving—as easily, efficiently and pleasurably as interaction between organism and environment can allow.

Human consumption is driving us to nuclear war, just as it's driving us to convert the Earth into a life system whose sole function is to feed humans. It's you and I that are bringing nuclear war on ourselves, not generals and politicians. Generals and politicians are playing their part. They're humans. And yes, because of their peculiar positions and functions, they contribute, as individuals, more to the pressure for nuclear war than you and I do. But whatever it is that generals and politicians peculiarly contribute to that pressure, I think we'd replace them if they didn't contribute it.

You and me. Hungry, lusty, greedy, egomaniacal, turned on, alive and stupefyingly resourceful, inventive and creative you and me. We consume. The bottom line of virtually everything we do is consumption. We consume because we *need* to consume. More more more. But there's only so much to consume. And everybody wants some.

We humans compete ferociously for what we want today. We compete every day in hosts of different contexts and configurations. We're each on hosts of different teams competing in different kinds of games simultaneously. Me, my family, gang, school, club, company, town, party, church, religion, class, race, country, socio-economic/ideological system, you name it, against you and yours.

We're all cooperating with each other to compete with each other. And the basic competitive unit isn't even the individual person. It's also my tough guy personality against my warm and generous, my Captain Get-It-All-Done against Sandy Weymouth, Anemic Sloth. It's not just all organisms against all other organisms. It's all their—our—multiple moods and personalities against each other and everybody else's. It gets *very* complicated.

The frenzy of human competition throughout the world is intensifying every second in septendecillions of ways and contexts. Television and the Internet not only provide a vivid picture of the frenzy, they energize our participation in it. Competition for access to your consciousness is frenzied, not just to imprint on it a product name, image and emotional association for when you're out shopping, but to get you to consume the product *now*, this instant. Mmm, brewski. Get it, pop it, chug-a-lug it *now*. I'd love to see the tobacco industry's statistics on how many lighters light up in cars passing the average cigarette billboard. Consume Now. And do the *only* thing you can when you run out: restock.

Digital media work a direct wire to our brain, stimulating consumption for about all we're worth. To get you to watch the ad, they have to get you to watch the show, and the competition is frenzied over what gets on for how long, who's in it and how to get you to watch it. The rewards are enormous for getting you to watch it, as they should be: your consumption is enormously rewarding.

On our side of the equation, the overwhelming majority of us are in frenzied competition for the money for all the stuff being sold. Hustle earn spend promote. We have met the frenzy and the frenzy is us.

The frenzy gets uglier out there in RealWorldLand. There it involves killing. *More* killing. Much more. Twenty-five million in wars since 1945, claims author Richard J. Barnet, and that was by 1983. A million in the Iran-Iraq war, many of them 13- and 14-year-old charging infantry"men", millions exterminated in Democratic Kampuchea, plus all the wars all over Southeast Asia, India, Afghanistan, the Middle East, Africa, Central America, and even Europe—Northern Ireland, Belgium, Hungary, Czechoslovakia, Poland, the former Yugoslavia, the former Soviet Union, the Persian Gulf, and on and on and on.

Frenzied human competition. Competition, I think, to consume. In some cases the basics—food, clothing, shelter—in others, much more. If all this consumption and competition is threatening our existence, why don't we—we affluents, at least—simply stop? Stop consuming. Stop competing. We've got enough to survive.

First, most of us don't know it's our consumption that's firing this frenzy whose climax is still likely to be nuclear war. Maybe I'm wrong. Maybe our consumption *isn't* firing the frenzy. Maybe the frenzy *won't* lead to nuclear war. And if I'm right, what am I supposed to do about it? If I stop consuming, how do I know anybody else will? All I do is miss what I want and make it easier for everybody else to get theirs. Terrific.

Pass laws? No more consumption? No more than a certain *amount* of consumption? Not likely. The political-economic systems we affluents are part of depend on constantly growing consumption, and much of what our governments do is aimed at achieving precisely that. A general curtailment of consumption in the affluent world could collapse the whole world card castle so apocalyptically that a good nuclear war as an alternative wouldn't look bad.

The answer, I believe, to the mess humanity is in lies not in restraining our consumption, our competition or anything else we want to do or get. Logic drives all the events of the universe. And I think logic dictates that sooner or later—maybe after many nuclear wars and Soylent Green ravagements of the Earth, from which life will relentlessly recover and re-elaborate—some technological species that will inevitably evolve will make the right move that gets that species past the logical imperatives for these traps.

But I want that species to be us. Now. No more war. No more ecological ravage. The right move *now*. Okay, here's the right move:

Part Three
Blossom

Fill yourself up. Get it all, do it all. All you want and need most. Total greed, total self-fulfillment. The second of two key points of this essay.

Do this and we'll all get over the hump and safely past the climax. We'll stop ravaging the Earth—I think we'll use less and less of it— and we'll avoid finally and forever destroying ourselves in a nuclear war. Conditions on Earth will be splendid. And we'll know it: in full cognizance we'll surrender to life, enriching it as we do.

It's what we want, isn't it? What we'd be totally greedy for if we thought about it? Think about it.

Life has reached its climax on Earth. At the climax of a life system, the cultural values essential to the stupendous success of the system's dominant, technological species must flip upside down. Only then will that species—humanity in our case—safely and permanently leave behind the apocalyptic dangers of the climax.

What was humanity's pre-climax value system, why did it work when it did, and why won't it work now? And what's the new, the post-climax value system? Why couldn't it work before? And why is it the only one that will work now, at and after the climax?

Control and restraint are the marrow of pre-climax values as I see them: hold back, rein in, deny yourself what you want and need

most. Hubris—to want too much, the supreme offense against the
gods, which they punish, for example, by melting the wax in Icarus'
fabricated wings when he flies too high and too close to the sun. Don't
fly too high is the message. Aristotelian moderation in all things: self-
restraint, self-discipline, in a word, self-distrust.

When we relate to other people, pre-climax values mean influencing, or trying to influence, other people. Control. An enormous
portion of human communication today and throughout the past is
people trying to get other people to feel, think, say and do what they
want them to: sh-sh baby, it's alright; put on your mittens, drink your
milk, do your homework, front and center, get a job, your attitude's
all wrong, you shouldn't feel that way, buy me, vote for me, *promise*
me. Why can't you keep your *promises*?

Hard to imagine a culture functioning without stuff like this,
isn't it? Are we supposed to stop telling our kids when to wear mittens? We'd stop if it meant stopping eco-ravage and nuclear war,
wouldn't we? Some incentive. But what's the connection? Mittens
and nuclear war?

Here's the connection. I believe we affluent humans consume as much
as we do because we're not getting fundamental, animal needs met.
And the more we satisfy these fundamental needs, the less we'll consume. And the less we consume, the less we'll ravage the Earth and
threaten ourselves with nuclear annihilation.

We're not getting fundamental, animal needs met because cultural controls prevent us, controls that enabled the culture we inherited
to emerge, survive and grow. Controls without which I don't think
any human culture could emerge, survive and grow. Any culture in
the past, that is.

Until now, control has been necessary for human culture to survive. Now control must disappear for us to continue to survive. That's

the argument. One simple reason for this flip is that throughout the past man has needed to grow, both in numbers and consumption. Now he needs *not* to grow. Ironic, isn't it—if it's true—that restraint has been key to human growth, while cut-her-loose and let-her-rip are key to reversing it? Reversing it peacefully, pleasurably and productively. Cut her loose and let her rip, many might reasonably fear, and our growth will reverse far too quickly and completely.

What are fundamental human needs, which ones have human cultures suppressed, and why?

Sex. First fundamental need to come to mind, right? About a light year ahead of whatever's next? That sex comes instantly to mind is considerable evidence it's a need that's suppressed. But who needs evidence? Does anyone doubt that all human cultures have restricted the sex drive? Severely? What's hard to imagine is a culture functioning and surviving against competitor cultures *without* restricting the sex drive. My suspicion is that before the climax of life no culture *can* survive and function without restricting it.

Why? Why has control of the sex drive been necessary to the success of human cultures? I think that, until sometime during the last 100 years, sexual repression grew with technology. The more advanced the technology, the broader and more effective the sex repression had to be.

Sex arouses intense feelings, have you noticed? Add to strictly sexual feelings the ones related to loyalty, jealousy and ownership that surround the issue of sexual access—in lots of species as well as our own—and you've got explosive potential for social disruption. The more advanced the technology, the more cooperation required of the individuals making it. And the more cooperation required, the more damage social disruption can cause, hence the greater need to control sex.

And until, again, sometime during the last 100 years, technology required population growth. The more advanced the technology, the more individuals required to do all the increasingly specialized things connected with making and using it. Various kinds of human groupings must have raced each other at population growth in order to beat competitors at exploiting technology's growing possibilities.

But the proliferation of fertility-promoting objects and rites in antiquity suggests that population growth wasn't as easy as the fun involved might suggest. Too much monkeying around with yourself or people of your own sex or people too young to reproduce isn't going to get population growth anywhere. And too much monkeying with close relatives won't do anything for your population's quality. You want vigorous, optimal-quality population growth, you need sex control.

And as advancing technology builds steeper hierarchies, sex becomes a strong card in getting up the hierarchy and staying there, a card you must therefore play with the greatest care and restraint to realize all its potential. Particularly when advancing technology is causing concepts of ownership to take hold with growing strength. What's the value of a dynastic marriage the central article of which has been traded all over town? Control your sex behavior or you'll piss away hierarchy opportunities.

Hey, you say, if advancing technology requires increasing sex repression, how come sex restrictions today are crumbling while technology streaks out of sight? While some might question how liberated we really are and how straitjacketed our forebears really were, I'm convinced that the sexual liberation of our generation is real. We're living, I think, in a unique period in the history of life when many things change. One change is that advancing technology's need for sex repression reverses.

The unique period is the climax of life on Earth, which I see as the climax of technology. The two are the same thing. Any life system progresses to a point at which the technology that inevitably occurs essentially fulfills its purpose. That purpose is to make the species developing it safer. At some point technology makes the species developing it as safe as it can. New developments may occur, but none that significantly improve the safety of the technological species.

Technology is always trying to spread. In its early stages it may be sticky and slow moving. Those who invent/discover, make and use technology obviously don't want to share it with those against whom they're using it to compete. Nevertheless, technology always spreads. People want to steal it, to learn or figure out its secrets, or buy them some way. To see a technological advantage anywhere is to want it and to do anything to get it. Survival against competition requires it.

Also, technology, as it advances, requires more people with more highly developed skills to produce it. This increases incentives to produce individual units of technology in larger quantities so that more people share its growing costs in human energy and skill. More people producing it, more people using it. Thus spreads technology.

Today, when information and communication is what technology is all about, the stuff's all over the place. Molasses has turned to water. Economist W. W. Rostow notes that significantly larger portions of university-age youth in such developing countries as mainland China, India and the Latin American countries are getting university level education. This, argues Rostow, is positioning these countries for much bigger stakes in the hi-tech world of the coming decades.

I don't think a technological species is optimally safe until *all* the safety technology can provide is equally accessible to *all* tech species members.

Competition for technology is dangerous. And like most dangers, I think technology eventually eliminates it. It's got to if two propositions

I've offered are valid. The first, that technology at some point saturates its ability to make its species safer, that it stops progressing—at least at providing safety. And second, that technology keeps on doing what it's always done: spreading, among steadily growing portions of the tech species (always, I'd claim, with growing speed). Given these two, the result is unavoidable: all species members eventually have access to all the safety technology can provide.

No way! you say. Technology is not reaching the impoverished Guatemalan *campesino* or the Ethiopian famine victim, and there's no indication it ever will.

If it weren't reaching them, retort I, they wouldn't be there. The reason so many humans are alive today is that enough technology to stay alive is reaching more of us than when we were fewer. No *Homo sapiens* can survive with anywhere near as little technology as even the most technological non-humans. So if any *Homo sapiens* is surviving, it's because of the relatively high level of technology he's got.

The question is whether *more* technology will get to the exploding numbers of the world's poor, enough for them to be as safe from death as we affluents are today; *or* as safe as anyone can ever be, the way I'm saying we affluents will be soon.

How does technology get to the world's poor now? Some they generate themselves. They make it, using existing technology: few humans, even the most primitive, make anything exclusively from resources not changed by other humans.

Some they earn, by supplying goods and services to those further inside technology's generative core. And much they are given, through government programs and institutional and individual generosity. Not a welcome implication: that generosity contributes to the world's population explosion and that more generosity will only enlarge the explosion.

So the question is whether the technology explosion will catch up with and pass the population explosion, possibly raising living standards or living standards expectations in some way that dampens population growth. In fact, that appears to be happening. Data derived from Colin McEvedy and Richard Jones's *Atlas of World Population History* (1978) and from more current sources indicate that human population growth rates, which *always* grew, began reversing at the end of the 19th century and have reversed in all parts of the world except central Africa. Populations are growing everywhere, but not as fast as they were. And long-term trends down in growth rates appear to be well established, even in most of the third world.

Many factors are working to spread technology through the vast perimeter of our species. Technology is getting cheaper (as always). The costs of resources are either remaining stable or dropping because of increased efficiency in resource use and growing abilities to find more of needed resources and to develop cheaper replacements. And communications technology is spreading like the wind: few people anywhere have not heard a radio or seen a cell phone, and most of them have seen vivid pictures of what mastery of modern technology and of population growth can bring them.

And there's generosity. I think humanity's vast perimeter could break off and succumb entirely to starvation, disease and violence without harming the material life of us hi-tech affluents. Such a development might even revitalize—like radical pruning—our material life. It certainly would the environment.

But it's not going to happen. We hi-tech affluents won't let it. We don't like suffering, and we give and vote a lot of money, time and energy to relieving it. We're generous. And the more powerful we become, the more generous we'll become, I believe. More on that later.

Today's *campesino* and famine victim may never see a computer. But their progeny will. They'll not just see them, they'll use them—computers and all the other splendors technology will have showered upon us.

So. If all the safety technology provides is equally accessible to all members of the technological species, gone then is the basis of the species' hierarchies. It's the extra safety that technology provides that makes some tech species members more powerful than others, puts them on top of others and thereby forms the hierarchies initially characteristic of a technological species. So it figures that, as technology becomes more fluid and harder for individuals to monopolize, as technology finally gets where it's really been flowing right from the beginning—to everybody—those hierarchies it formed like crystals have to disintegrate. We all become equal again, the way we were before technology took off. The only difference now is that each of us is as safe as any organism in that environment, in that life system, can ever be.

And with no hierarchies, gone is the motive to consume all that stuff we needed to get *up* hierarchies, and stay up them. Identity consumption, $180,000 Porsche and stuff—what I believe makes up most of the cost of what we affluents consume today—identity consumption is history.

And if tech species members are optimally safe from physical threats from their environment and free of feelings generated by hierarchies and getting and staying up them, then consumption aimed at controlling feelings—caffeine, nicotine, alcohol, drugs—is history too. Or at least it's radically reduced. And if identity and feelings-control consumption are either history or radically reduced, so then is a significant portion of overall consumption.

But there's a problem. Consumption not only fuels accelerating eco-ravage and the drive to nuclear war, it also fuels technological advancement. Where does technology go if people don't consume its products? Nowhere. And without technological advancement, how can all the safety of technology reach all humans? It can't. And if no technology spread among all humans, then no elimination of hierarchy, no radical reduction of consumption and thus of eco-ravage and pressure for nuclear war, no chicken, no egg, no climax, no nothin'. How do you get the whole thing started?

Like everything in nature, the climax of technology is not marked by nice clear lines. It isn't a point on a graph. It's a curve. And I think some of the benefits of the climax start kicking in as soon as the curve starts, which might be long before the actual climax, the *climax* of the climax.

I think the curve of the technological climax starts when technology starts spreading so much faster than anybody can keep it from spreading that the hierarchies—which technology until then has been making steeper the faster it advances—stop getting steeper so fast and eventually stop getting steeper at all and flatten out.

I think this has already started to happen on Earth. Sometime around the end of the Victorian Age the speed with which hierarchies in the advanced western countries got steeper peaked. They may still be getting steeper, but not as fast as they were, and not at rates remotely comparable to today's technology explosion.

Long term studies of wealth and income distribution in the U.S. and England by economists Peter H. Lindert and Jeffrey G. Williamson support this view. Inequalities of wealth and income distribution, they find, grew much more rapidly in these countries during the second half of the 19th century than during periods that preceded (their data goes back to 1774 for the U.S. and to 1670 for England). And these inequalities, furthermore, stabilized in the first half of the twentieth century and declined afterwards.

Many claim that wealth and income inequalities resumed growth in the U.S. in the 1980s. I'd argue that a spurt followed decades of government efforts to reduce inequalities by redistributing wealth and income. The Reagan administration curtailed these programs to some extent during the '80s, believing that they sapped the very economic vitality necessary to improve everyone's quality of life.

The long-term global trend, I claim, is toward equalization. For everybody. Hierarchies are in the early stages of flattening out of existence. Flattening *up* out of existence. Mass aristocracy. And technology, not government action, is making it happen.

And as technology continues to streak out of sight, people are getting safer. *Safer*, you say? Isn't eco-ravage and nuclear war kind of a tip-off that technology gets more dangerous as it advances? Sure. The more powerful technology is and the more power and safety it gives its user, the more dangerous it is. Most of the history of technology is about converting immediate and specific dangers to remote and general ones. But that process, I think, reverses late in the climax, leaving us afterwards with all the safety of technology and few, if any, of the dangers. More on that later.

Either way, there's no doubt in my mind that we affluents today are incredibly safe. We could be safer, and I think we will be. But take an honest look down your hierarchy or back down technological or biological evolution and you'll see how much *un*safer we could be.

Now you'd think with all this safety, we affluents could worry less about hierarchies. I'm safe, the hell with climbing and staying up hierarchies. Or at least putting any more energy into climbing and staying than is absolutely necessary. And less energy in climbing and staying up hierarchies should mean less identity consumption. And more safety—from the nonhuman environment and the hierarchy competition of the human environment—should mean less feelings-control consumption. And drops in identity and feelings-control consumption should leave us that much closer to consuming only what we really want and need. In other words, increased safety should mean more *focused* consumption.

This more focused consumption could be adequate to drive technology forward in the areas where we really need it, namely, knocking out remaining safety threats and providing more pleasure. I mean do we really need more breakthroughs in fashion cosmetics? Mood-altering agents? Porsches? These are pleasures! you say. No they're not. Vehicles to pleasure maybe. *Perceived* vehicles. Go for the real stuff and I think you'll park this junk back in the dumpster.

Solution to the problem. Increasingly focused consumption resulting from growing safety and technology's accelerating efficiency should, by reducing *overall* consumption, get us safely past eco-ravage and nuclear war, past the climax of technology to the millions, indeed billions, of years of Nirvana Utopia Heaven that lie beyond.

But Nirvana Utopia Heaven doesn't seem to be the track we're on, does it? While we affluents are getting safer and safer from just about everything, we're still identity and feelings-control consuming our buns off. And we're threatening each other and harming other life forms faster every minute to do it. Overall consumption is going up, not down. Its *growth rate* is going up, not down. Why?

It's the old value system, I think. The one we used to need. Control, hubris, Icarus, put on your mittens, moderation in all things, self-discipline, self-deprivation, self-distrust. *These* ancient and venerable values are making us buy all this identity and mood-altering crap? These puritan values are driving today's out-of-control mass consumption frenzy? I think they are.

I think these values are preventing us from meeting our deepest animal needs, needs that earlier humans simply had to forego to contribute to the advance of their technology and to enjoy its benefits. To survive, in other words. Increasingly, because the climax of technology has started, we don't need to deny ourselves these needs. To the extent we do, we overconsume.

Climax of technology 2

Again, what are your basic needs? Pretty subjective question: meet the needs you're aware of and you discover new ones. Here are some I've discovered in me that I imagine to be shared by most humans.

1. Sex, of course. It's the best. It's the best especially when you're doing it with the person you love the best. So they say and so I believe. Maybe this is a need most are pretty good at meeting. You tell me. I'm not.

2. Intense, rich, intimate interaction with other people. With or without sex. I'm better at that. The without part. Talk talk talk. Best times of my life. Ideas, self-revelations, arguments, clownings. It's a basic I want a lot more of, with *and* without.

3. Nurturing, cuddling, holding. A couple of years ago after starting to write this, I wanted some therapy. Parks had died by this time, so I went to an old friend from Parks' groups in whose communal family I'd lived for a while. Joan Goldberg, Brooklyn, New York. Joan's in her early 60s and does re-parenting therapy. She provides physical and emotional nurturing which she believes few if any of us get enough of when we're young. I curl up between her legs like a fetus, she sitting on a bed, my head in her lap, both of us naked (my idea), she scratching my back, sides and arms (also my idea; I love being scratched, kind of hard).

Nurturing, cuddling, holding, touching, scratching, rubbing, prefera-
bly naked, with or without, it's basic, I think. Not just nice. We need it.

4. Family, tribe, herd. We need to be part of an intimate net-
    work that validates and strengthens us, that gives us material
    and emotional support to survive and flourish in life. And I
    think this need runs a lot deeper than what we get from the
    20th century novelty, the Nuclear Family. No hand-wringer
    I over the break-up of the American family. Good riddance.
    Unless we haven't got anything better, which we don't. Yet.

The American family: too few people trying to get too many fundamental needs met by too few others. An impossible tyranny on parents. Too much consumption, too much control, too much screen
time. Only the best things life can offer can lure us away from the
screen. I'm describing those things now—my conception of them—
and I think they're damned hard to find in or via the nuclear family.

Mayhem. Happy mayhem. *Mostly* happy mayhem. Wrestling,
chasing, games, made-up-on-the-spot games, flirting, teasing, laugh-
ing scheming cheating sweating heated up red in the face, boys girls,
kids grownups. Crying. Screaming. And then intense, heavy talk.
Intense rich interaction with other people. And animals. People and
animals that live where I do. Family. It's a basic human need, I think.
And key to family is kids. They're basic too. Lifestyles they're not in
(mine now, for instance) don't interest me much.

5. I often wonder, if you didn't teach kids what you thought they
    ought to learn, but just got behind their learning what they
    wanted to learn when they wanted to learn it, taught them
    what they told you to teach them, what order would they
    learn things in. I think kids would spend much more time

than they're allowed to now just learning how to operate their bodies. Chasing, escaping, fighting, climbing, balancing, imitating other people, doing it all more and more gracefully, dancing.

Moving the body, improving its strength and skills, mastering fun things to do with it, feeling its powers and skills grow, I think all this is a basic human need, and not just when we're kids.

6. If kids determine their own learning schedule, they'll never learn to read or write, will they? I think there are two reasons kids *will* learn to read and write, even if nobody pushes them to. The key assumption is that somebody is always there to teach them what they want to learn when they want to learn it.

First, kids, like all organisms, want to survive, and they want the quality of their survival to be as high as possible. I think reading and writing are vital to the survival of the cultures that use those skills and thus of most individuals in those cultures. If that's the case, learning the connection between reading, writing and surviving is hard to miss, since, presumably, you stop surviving if you don't learn it. In a way, this is the reasoning used to impose reading and writing on children. Force them to read and write or they won't. Force them to survive or they won't.

The other reason kids will learn to read and write, I think, is that learning is fun, using your brain is fun, communicating and saving information—e.g. reading and writing—exploring, discovering, creating and using your brain to do it all, it's all intensely fun. Impose knowledge on people and you neutralize the fun of exploring and discovering. Teach when and what you're asked to by the learner—otherwise let them discover it and make it their own. Optimal educational efficiency: they'll learn it fastest and it'll stick best. Because using the brain is a fundamental human pleasure and need.

7. Love. A basic human need. Being important, special to another or others. Being a turn-on, a stimulus, a source of excitement to another or others, someone they need to see and get next to regularly. Not the shock concept of the essay: we need this, all of us, and I daresay very few of us get anywhere near enough of it.

8. And feelings. We need to experience our feelings. Totally. We want to, and we want to because it's a fundamental human animal organism need to. And vast quantities of what human culture is about prevent us from, or at least help us avoid, experiencing our feelings. Human culture that thousands, millions of years of predecessors put in place. If they hadn't, we probably wouldn't be around to complain about it.

SEX
INTIMACY
NURTURING
FAMILY
BODY ACTION
MIND ACTION
LOVE
FEELINGS

And survival. Like all organisms, humans need to survive, a need to which all others defer. What all others are *about*.

So how are we doing? Are we fulfilling any of these needs enough? Anywhere near as much as we want? If you think we are, you're reading the wrong book.

I think human cultures in the past have had to restrict fulfillment of all these needs for several reasons. I've already argued that, prior to the technological climax, three things increasingly restrict sexual feelings and behavior: advancing technology's need for social cooperation, its need for population growth, and the hierarchies that technology inevitably forms in cultures developing it. And I've argued that acting out *any* feelings, sexual or otherwise, can disrupt the cooperation that technology requires of those exploiting it.

I think technology requires four cultural characteristics which conflict with fulfillment of basic human needs. The more technology advances—up to a point—the more it requires these characteristics:

SOCIAL COOPERATION
POPULATION GROWTH
CONSUMPTION GROWTH
GROWING HIERARCHIES

Actually, advancing technology doesn't *require* growing hierarchies the way it requires the other three. Hierarchies are just the inevitable product of technology and competition. Any organism would do anything to maximize its superiority over competitors—which is what humans do with technology when they get it, and why social hierarchies result.

But technology doesn't *require* that technological cultures form hierarchies, for example, to organize the flow of human energy and skill to advance and exploit the technology. If technology does require hierarchies, why isn't technological advancement falling into disarray as hierarchy growth slows? I think data indeed indicates that hierarchy growth is slowing. And it's self-evident to me that technology is not falling into disarray, that it continues to streak ahead with quantum-leaping speed and force.

Hierarchies, because they grow, are the medium in which human energy and skills flow. They're the instrument that orders and organizes the energy and skills. But that doesn't mean they're necessary to do it. We may—I think we will—find that human energy and skill can be organized just as well, if not better, without hierarchies. Decentralized, "matrix" management and the spread of "quality circles" in manufacturing can be viewed, I think, as trends toward reduced hierarchy in the world's business enterprises. And if they are trends, they are so because they make the enterprises work better: competing businesses can't afford to do things to be nice.

Four characteristics of technological culture conflict with fulfillment of basic human needs. Which is why technological cultures on the go must increasingly suppress these needs. And if your culture isn't on the go, it's going to get eaten up by ones that are.

Love for instance. Not all love generates or nurtures population growth. You've got to love a fertile member of the opposite sex and you've got to express that love in ways that produce progeny. None of that nasty non-progeny-producing stuff. And loving someone who "belongs" to someone else can disrupt social cooperation. Generally the same rules—and reasons for them—as for sex. Control love. Restrain it. Send it in the right directions. If love doesn't go in the right directions or come from them, then block it. Stop it.

Prior to the technological climax, the social cooperation that technology requires restricts what an individual can do with his or her mind and body. Cultures that most successfully control what their members do with their minds and bodies coordinate best the diverse activities that advancing technology is generating. I think technological culture in the late Victorian era imposed conformity of all kinds more successfully—the individual internalized it more deeply—than it would ever, before or after. Which meant maximum restrictions on what you could do with your mind and body. And maximum pressure to do what you could do *hard*. *Produce*, Jack, if you want to survive. If you want your family, company, country to survive. To survive you've got to *prevail.*

Are we as "intimate" as we can be? As we want to be? Have we been meeting that need? To me, intimate means letting others know what you really think, feel, want and need. And letting them reveal that to you. Emotional closeness.

I think we're not as intimate as we could be, as we want to be—nowhere near—because our identities get in the way. Our lifetime project of making ourselves into a this or a that, building credibility in ourselves and others for this identity. Hell, we may even *become* the identity.

Definitive phoney, right? Well, by definition I guess it is. But it's not frivolous, unnecessary phoney. Identity is necessary to survival. It's a response to competition. As technology elaborates, hierarchies grow, up which we have to climb. And identifying ourselves is vital to a successful climb.

But identity blocks direct emotional contact. Projecting an identity—for entirely valid survival reasons—is a different process than simply being what we really are at any given moment. Like it or not, survival in hierarchies requires identity projection more than emotional closeness. And when hierarchies are what you're in, not surviving in them is not surviving at all.

Physical contact with other people, contact that nurtures, and the all-the-way healer/energizer, *naked* physical contact, do we get it? Enough? From enough people? From enough *important* people? People important to us? No way. Too close to sex. I mean where do you draw the line? Of course, we do draw the line—back at about shaking hands. Don't get near that disgusting sex stuff. That cooperation-disrupting sex stuff. Whatever represses our sex needs represses our needs for nurturing physical contact.

Family. Technology makes families smaller and smaller. Down from tribes to biological families with close connections with other ones, down to fairly autonomous extended families, down to, yuck, the nuclear family. Advancing technology increasingly requires suppression of feelings. Families generate feelings. So make the family smaller so it doesn't generate so much feeling.

Throughout history people have grabbed every opportunity to live in greater relative isolation, i.e. in living units where fewer other people live. The mass affluence that technology produced during the 20th century offered an isolation bonanza. We can surround ourselves with *things*, and thereby get people out of our faces. And we can use *things* to be autonomous, so we don't need the people we're isolating from. Our own house, our own lawn, my own room, bathroom, sound system, TV, computer, telephone. You watch: within the decade, every kid'll have his own mini-refrigerator/freezer and microwave. *Never* see him. Her. No contact, no feelings, perfect.

So smaller families feed technology's need not only for feelings suppression but also for consumption. Everybody's got to have his own everything. People who share don't consume.

Four requirements of technology

> SOCIAL COOPERATION
>
> POPULATION GROWTH
>
> CONSUMPTION GROWTH
>
> GROWING HIERARCHIES

separate us from our deepest needs—until the climax of technology. Then everything changes.

How does that work? What does the climax of technology do to each of these four that lets humans fulfill their deepest needs and, as a result, consume less?

Okay, I've already covered one of the four. I've claimed that hierarchy turnaround *defines* the beginning of the climax. Technology gets so fluid that tech species members can't hold on to it the way they used to. They can't monopolize it as much, can't use it as much to get on top of each other and build social hierarchies. Growing segments of the tech species gain more and more access to more and more technology. So the hierarchies that technological exclusivity used to form stop getting steeper and start getting flatter.

As I say, I think wealth and income distribution trends indicate that human hierarchies have stopped getting steeper as fast as they used to. I think they're going to stop getting steeper at all and start to flatten. Flatten *up*. By the climax of the climax—in a hundred or so years, when all humans will have equal access to most technology—hierarchies will have flattened up virtually out of existence. If that's the case, hierarchies are one needs-suppressing characteristic of tech cultures that the technological climax removes. That the *start* of the climax *starts* to remove.

And if that's the case, then less hierarchy should mean less suppression of sex needs: you use and control sex less to get and stay up the hierarchy if there's less hierarchy to get and stay up. Same with love. The less hierarchy there is, the less you're going to restrict your love targets and sources to those who can help you get and stay up the hierarchy.

And less sex control should mean less suppression of our needs for nurturing physical contact. So it leads to sex. You may be taking your life in your hands, but not any hierarchy position or ambitions. (And I don't think sex is always going to be as dangerous as it's been in the last decade. Either we'll cure AIDS, we'll prevent it, or we'll become more adept at avoiding it without compromising sexual fulfillment.)

Finally, less hierarchy should mean less identifying, more opening up and "just being," and thus more emotional closeness, more intimacy.

Population growth. As noted earlier, human population growth rates began reversing toward the end of the 19th century. Growth rates which always grew, from as far back as estimates exist, have almost everywhere stopped growing and started to decline.

The first question is why did human populations always grow faster. The answer, I think, is that technological development is inherently an accelerating process. It snowballs. The more technology you've got, the more you can make. At least up to a point—a point we haven't reached yet. The more technology you've got, the more pieces you can mix together into new technology—or that *your* technology can mix into new technology.

And as technology snowballs, it allows *and requires* the population making and using it to snowball, to grow faster and faster, until the beginning of the climax.

The second question is why have these population growth rates reversed? And why did they start to reverse at the beginning of the technological climax? In other words, at the same time hierarchy growth started to reverse? Does the growth of a species that's developing technology accelerate until the climax starts and then reverse and decelerate? The numbers suggest it does. If so, why?

The answer, I think, has to do with technology's contribution to its own making and advancing. Right from its infancy, technology contributes to its own making and advancing. You need a second stone to make an Oldowan chopper. You can't put an edge on a stone with your bare hands (or even your head). From there on up, you need technology to make technology. The more advanced it is, the more technology you need to advance it. At some point technology contributes so much to its own making and advancing that it spews new technology *without* needing what it always needed before to do it: rising rates of population growth.

What reverses technology's need for accelerating population growth? Puberty does, I think. Technology puberty. At some indefinable time technology gathers enough momentum to swing into high gear, into a gigantic growth spurt. Nothing specific like hormones triggers it. Everything is just in place, and when it is, it's got to happen: steam power, railroads, powered ships of steel, telegraph, telephones, cars, radios, airplanes, TVs, nuclear power, computers, robotization, DNA manipulation, space travel.

Like all puberty, technology's doesn't last long. On Earth it started maybe 150 years ago. And as I say, I think it'll be over in about a hundred years. Not long compared to its several million-year childhood.

But why does tech puberty drive *down* tech species population growth rates? Why doesn't it drive them that much higher?

Because technology's ability to contribute to its own making and advancing is what explodes during tech puberty. I think technology's contribution, relative to that of the tech species, is always growing, right from the beginning. Relative to the human contribution in time and energy, technology's contribution to weaving a rug is much greater than to putting an edge on an Oldowan chopper. Same for making a rocket compared to weaving the rug. Maybe our species will eventually contribute nothing: all just robots, who knows?

When tech puberty hits, technology really starts growing, much faster than ever before. And multiplying its contribution to its own advancement is what all this growth is about. So that technology's soaring contribution drives down the tech species' relative contribution much harder and faster than it did earlier. So much harder and faster that the species' population growth rates—which had to grow to support technological advancement *even while* the species' relative contribution to that advancement always declined—now have to slow down, stop growing altogether and start dropping.

But how do those populations contributing most to the making and advancing of technology find out their contribution isn't needed as much as it used to be? How do technology's needs translate to tech species needs?

For one thing, there's a job squeeze. Technology is taking over job opportunities. Also, tech species members are complicated, so technology has to be complicated to replace them. By the time technology has gotten that complicated, it takes a lot of training to contribute to it. Arm and a leg to train your kid to contribute enough to technology to earn a hierarchy position comparable to the one he/she was born in.

Now I think the time is coming when kids will learn what they want to learn when they want to learn it. Massively improved interaction with computers will play a big role there. As a result, kids will learn much more, they'll learn it better, and it'll cost virtually nothing to do it.

But the low cost of education won't induce tech species members to have more kids. For one thing, the job situation won't get any better. And they won't *need* kids. Safety is what all this technology spewing itself out is all about. The more so, generally, the higher you are in the hierarchy. And the safer you are, the less you need offspring. *Safer*? Tech species members have offspring for *safety*? It's a big reason, I think.

Offspring make valuable allies in competition, starting long before they reach adulthood. Helpers, workers, maybe even fighters. You need all the protection you can get, to keep your accumulated wealth, for example. Even at the bottom of the hierarchy, fully functional people usually accumulate wealth as they grow older. Not much, necessarily, but more than what they started with.

And poor people can't afford to protect their wealth the way rich people can. Maybe the rich help the poor a little on this score—subsidies for police, for example (which also keep the poor in line)—but never to where the poor get the level of protection the rich get. I mean, what's the point of getting rich? So if you're way down the hierarchy, you might have to bear two handfuls of offspring to get a handful of protectors, i.e. males—maybe more before you get the kind of males who can actually protect you.

But the more advanced technology is and the further up the hierarchy you are, the less you need the help and protection of a big family. Technology provides it.

Why does growth of the technological species start to reverse at the same time hierarchy growth does? Because both are caused by the same thing: technology puberty.

The same tech puberty that drives down the tech species' relative contribution to technology so fast and hard that population growth rates reverse also pumps out technology so fast that tech species members can't control it the way they used to. As a result, they can't get the competitive advantages which such control used to offer, and as a result of that, the hierarchies such advantages form have to crumble. Crumble *up*. So in fact, both hierarchy reversal *and* population growth reversal characterize the beginning of the technological climax.

Okay, so population growth is another of technology's needs that starts to reverse at the beginning of the technological climax. Freeing us to fulfill more completely what basic human needs? Well, if the population growth imperative blocked sex, nurturing and love needs as I argued it did, reversing it ought to free them up.

Okay, sex. Now, how did that go? Eliminate technology's need for population growth and you're free to monkey with yourself, others of your own sex and, uh-oh, close relatives. Doesn't sound so good, does it?

Woods Place

Here's what I want to do when I get this book done: buy some land, 30, 40 acres, off the beaten track so I can afford it, but not more than a few hours from a major city. I want mostly woods. I like the insulation from the weather, cool in the summer, warm in the winter. (Ever notice how winter's warmer inside a woods than outside?) The air's nice in the woods, all those leaves photosynthesizing carbon dioxide into fresh oxygen. And noise insulation: I want people to scream and carry on if they like, loud as they like, loud as *we* like. Conversely, I want to insulate from lawn mowers, weed-eaters, buzz-saws, all the stuff that makes a suburban summer sound like a hyperactive dentist's office. I want to insulate from the roar and stink of the highway, from internal combustion generally.

Woods is what happens if you leave the land alone, at least it is in much of the U.S. I'd like to see humans leave more land alone, suburban lawn land for openers. *Some* open space, of course, for growing food, and for fun—wrestling, Frisbee, stuff like that. Lawn, maybe, but much less per capita than in suburbia where it's hardly used at all.

The first thing I want to build in the Woods Place is a wants/needs board. There I want to post my wants and needs. The first of which will be that other people post their wants and needs, if they want to. I plan to watch the board for opportunities to give other people what they want and need most. Giving precisely what others want most now is one of my top turn-ons. Even material stuff, though I may not give a lot of that. What's left? Emotional work: support in processing feelings completely, physical nurturing possibly, support in your doing and getting what you want and need most.

Giving is power. When it's what the recipient wants or needs most, it's power for the recipient. And what a charge, what power, to contribute to other people's power, to their learning, their ability to grow faster and do and get more of what they want. I love the power giving gives *me*, like giving a plant what it needs and seeing the results.

I can imagine a lot of human economics working this way in the future. Not soon. Publicize your wants and needs, and give people what you want to give them: see what *they've* publicized. No shoulds, musts or have to's. Give when it's a turn-on, when it's fun to, when it's what you want to do most. Maybe by the end of my life I'll be meeting most of my needs this way. Until then, I'll give what I want, take what I get, and work somehow to earn the rest.

My second request on the wants/needs board will be for help building a starter dwelling, starter in the sense that I hope others follow. The main space inside the dwelling could be any size, divided in half, one side being a platform about waist high with mattresses and pillows, surrounded on all three sides by windows. Like a bed, wider than it is long, that takes up half the room no matter how big the room is.

I'd want enough room on the platform so a fairly large group could sit and lean back against the wall below the windows. You eat, sleep, talk and you-know-what on the platform. You live there. Many can. The platform allows people to sit as close to or, within obvious limits, as far from each other as they want. Couches and chairs prejudice that choice, stuffed armchairs particularly—a literal instance of material luxury separating people.

The other half of the main space would be a hard wood floor where you can dance, jump around and carry on, and stomp back and forth and gesticulate while addressing people on the platform. You could put conventional furniture in this space when visitors come who are too weirded out by sitting and eating up on a platform.

No delicate things around. Nothing a toddler can hurt. Or that can hurt toddler. Toddlers are more important than things. And here toddlers do what they want.

Also in the dwelling are kitchen, bathroom, laundry and storage space. I might have a smaller but similar dwelling elsewhere in the woods, no kitchen for instance, for being alone. Or alone with. Being alone when you want is vital—particularly with a lot of infants and toddlers around.

What I want to do in the Woods Place is support people doing and getting what they want and need most. I'd like to see groups develop, like a non-stop round-the-clock group you can join and leave whenever you want. Groups where people can scream and cry, jump around and carry on. Or experience feelings silently, or just talk. And snuggle, naked if they want. Groups where people feel safe, if that's what they want to feel.

I want to see people support each other and experience feelings that come up along the way, feelings that keep them from supporting each other, for instance. The theory being, when people experience their feelings, they get past them, get more of what they want, and support others in getting more of what *they* want. Supporting people is fun for me, and I think it is, or would be, for others. A bunch of people supporting each other and you've got a kind of breeder reactor: Bang, Power.

As far as I'm concerned, people can come to the Woods Place when they want and stay as long as they want: five minutes, three weeks, rest of their lives. If it gets crowded, maybe we can find more land to use and spread, like a contagion. And, as far as I'm concerned, people can leave when they want and come back when they want. Five minutes, three weeks, never. No commitments.

I'm not wild about commitment. I like people to be around me because they like me, because I'm a turn-on for them, not because they're committed. And vice versa, because they're a turn-on for me. Vows of love I don't need. Declarations—when they're what you feel most like declaring—great. I like seeing people do things because they're turned on to them. They do better what they're turned on to than what they're committed to, don't you think? I won't mind when I've seen my last stiff upper lip.

I'd like to see a family develop in the Woods Place: twenty-five, fifty people, that range, fair portion of kids.

But wait, you say. Communal living didn't work in the late 60s and early 70s, why is it going to work now? Who says it didn't work? I do. It didn't draw a growing portion of the general population to a form of social organization that I think offers critical advantages both to the individual and to human culture as a whole.

What are these critical advantages? People pooling time, energy and money on food, for one. As far as I'm concerned, the Woods Place is DoWhatYouWantLand, so if you want to grow, purchase, transport, prepare, eat and clean up after your own food, be my guest. I don't want to. You take care of my food, I'll take care of your feelings, that's what I want. I don't expect to get it, but I'd like to be part of a fair amount of resource pooling in this area. Feed more people with less time, energy and money. And more fun: I like eating with other people, varieties of them. When I don't want to, I won't.

I think group living will make it easier to pool responsibility for kids. Pool it among all the kids' parents, other adults—ones like me without kids who are dying for involvement with them—and among other kids, assuming they're interested, which I think they usually will be. Result? Much more freedom for the individual parent. Less pressure, less confinement. Less money, maybe *no* money, spent on baby sitters and day care.

And kids living in a group have more than one or two parents to go to for information, praise, cuddling, and comfort from fear or pain. More adults with whom they can form close attachments. Adults they live with, who are available a lot of the time. Maybe more than their parents.

I like lots of kids living together. The intensity of interaction, the energy they feed each other, energy that can reach great heights and that I think enrich and empower children. *Assuming* older people are around for averting real danger. And for nurturing and providing emotional support when high kid energy or anything else causes fear or pain.

I'd welcome a community where children are more the responsibility of the community as a whole and less that of the biological parent. Again, this is DoWhatYouWantLand. I'm not interested in taking anything away from parents they don't ravenously desire to give up. I only plan to post on the wants/needs board that I want to look after some kids. "Be my guest" is the choral response I anticipate. What I'm after is that parents be relieved—precisely to the extent they want to be—of the horrific, round-the-clock burdens of contemporary child-rearing, burdens that poison the rightfully expected joys of having children. I'd like to see these burdens picked up by others who want them and by the efficiencies of responsibility pooling.

Another critical advantage to group living: common safety. I sometimes think major resistance to firearms control comes from people holed up with their little nuclear families in their isolated suburban forts, scared. I think if you're living with a fairly large number of people at least most of whom you experience as family, you, your children, your property are objectively and significantly safer from accident and crime.

The practical pluses of group living. Beyond them is an appeal that runs deeper in me, and I think in many others. It's a primal yearning to belong to something, a herd, a tribe, something reasonably permanent, involving a fair number of people. People that we like, a lot, people who are important to us and—critically—to whom *we* are important. It's a yearning, I believe, that's nowhere near filled by living with a child or two or three, or with another adult and a child or two or three.

Fluidity and plurality have become big words for me. I think people need in a lifetime more than two parents, a couple of siblings, one spouse and a couple of offspring. Living in a group can enable kids to have lots of siblings and lots of friends to choose from and switch among, whom they live with rather than just see in school. For adults: confine your sex to one other if you want, for life if you want. It's DoWhatYouWantLand. But a much larger family, I'm convinced, will provide much more room to move and choose and, therefore, meet all wants and needs much more completely. And—key point—it's not DoWhatYouWantLand if you can't be alone when and for as long as you want.

If group living's appeal can run so deep, why didn't it stick in the 60s? What did 60s communards do or not do that kept their group living efforts from enjoying broader and more enduring success?

I don't know. I'm fairly sure they did or tried to do a lot of things I don't want to do. And I don't think they tried to do one thing I do want to do—at least not to the extent I want to do it. And I think my combination will work.

I don't want to be self-sufficient, for instance. I don't want to grow my own food and clothes. If people want to grow some food—I'll probably grow *some* food, help grow some—or make some of their own clothes, if they want to try to be self-sufficient, I'll probably support it. As I claimed earlier, if the apocalypse that 60s communards thought they were preparing for by being self-sufficient were actually to occur—collapse of the hi-tech culture we're *all* part of—the sane among us would beg anybody with nukes to pop us out of our misery.

The size of a technological species' econiche, and therefore population, is determined by the level of advancement of the species' technology. Drop technology from what it is today to that of, say, the mid-18th century and the world's human population would have to drop by about 7/8ths, or say, 6 billion, to get down to what technology then supported. And you can be sure the 1/8th that's left will be dominated—as is always the case in pre-industrial cultures—by warriors, not by growers, fixers and tinkerers. The latter will grow, fix and tinker for the warriors, who'll war for control over land, trade routes, growers, fixers and tinkerers.

Not only am I not in rebellion against high technology, I'm convinced that it's one of the two keys that will enable group living to work successfully (emotional work, of course, is the other). Small, inexpensive computers and cell phones, through their communications and accounting capabilities, for example, will greatly enhance group living's ability to work smoothly and efficiently. Hooked up to the outside world, computers will bring good income into relatively remote places like the Woods Place, assuming you've developed marketable talents whose products can be transmitted electronically.

I don't believe, as I think people have for decades, that technology's ultimate destiny is to transform humans into clones and our environment into plastic. Sterilization and dehumanization is not where technology is taking us and it never was.

I envision technology increasingly freeing humans to be what we yearn most to be—what we particularly yearned to be in the late 60s and early 70s—more organic, more natural, more complete. I think the reason the 60s didn't work better is that technology wasn't advanced enough. I see technology as an increasingly thin membrane that will enable us, for example, to live as long and close to nature in the wild as we want without having to play the deadly game from which nature in the wild can't escape.

Similarly, I think technology in the long run will free us to be more organic, natural and complete in our relations with each other. I'd maintain it's been doing that for quite a while. Take an honest look back through the generations you've had contact with. We're closer, more open and more authentic, our relations are much richer than those of earlier generations. Technology did that? Largely, I think. And it's going to do it more.

I'm not in rebellion against money and materialism. I want to have all I want and need and let my consumption drop off afterward. More more more. No end to what I'll want, given the wherewithal, right? Not, I think, if I focus on *and get* what I want most.

Pooled property and income don't interest me. Give what you want to give when you want to give it, that's my ideal. Obviously, team up with anybody on anything, like growing, purchasing and preparing food, and you'll have to contribute equitably to partake equitably. Logic. I'd like people at the Woods Place to let go of any possessions and income only when and because they want to. "Give what you can and take what you need," said Marx. Not for me thanks. Give what you want and take what you get. If you don't like what you get, give it away.

Commitment. You can't have a commune that works without commitment. The history of communes—a history reaching well back into our own colonial period and back thousands of years elsewhere in the world—is unequivocal on this point. The more committed the commune to political, philosophical or religious principles, the longer it survives, with the religious ones coming out squarely on top.

Well, I'm for a commune that doesn't work, then, because I'm going into mine committed to as few principles as I can get away with. Here they are: Me. Me having fun. The most, best fun I can. Me achieving the highest, deepest, richest, most complete fulfillment I can.

Sex, that's all you're after, Weymouth. No it's not. I am after it, and I'd like to cover this subject in the detail it deserves in the next section.

My commitment is not to group living. Me, my fun, my fulfillment, that's my commitment. And experiencing feelings that get in the way, getting them out of the way. Experience convinces me I'll have fun getting behind others getting what they want, behind the feelings that get in *their* way. And maybe *they'll* get the fun and fulfillment I've gotten from this. Chain reaction. Contagion. Contagion that consumes humanity.

This is emotional work. And emotional work is what I don't think the communards of the 60s took into their communes, at least not to the extent I want to take it into mine. Fun and fulfillment, experiencing feelings, getting behind others, chain reaction contagion, I think out of all this will evolve the best ways to live. We'll never find better ways, and we'll never want to. And I think these best ways will involve most people living most of the time in groups larger and more complex than what we live in now, living that way because that's how we'll want most to live.

Now most of you reading this are about as drawn to group living as you are to setting yourselves on fire. I'm for your doing and getting what you want most (please don't set yourself on fire), and if putting as much distance as possible between you and living with more than the bare minimum of others is what you want, I totally support it.

My conviction is that group living that grows out of emotional work—and that optimally exploits available technology—will work so well economically and emotionally that you'll be pulled in. You'll want it. And if you don't, your children or your grandchildren will.

And it wouldn't have to be in the woods or even the country. Urban, suburban, you-name-it EW group living setups should work fine if they work anywhere. Key pieces, as I see them, are the wants/needs board and a 'kiva,' a term I'm stealing from southwestern Native American culture. For me, the kiva is an enclosed, sound-proofed space with mattresses and pillows where you can surrender to feelings, scream, cry, where you'll likely find someone to give you cuddles, intimacy, whatever you need the most. Sex? Maybe. You work that out and, again, more on that later.

Here's the kicker on group living. It's a stretch, and it won't happen tomorrow. But I think this form of social organization will be *the* vehicle for declines in both human population and, much more important, human consumption. Not just declines in growth rates, declines in actual numbers and amounts. Radical retrenchment of the human presence on Earth. Safe, fun, productive retrenchment, nobody gets squeezed.

Here's how I think it'll work. People living in groups will want to have children of their own less than people not living in them. And not because their lives are infested with kids. If they feel that way, I'd say they haven't learned how to get what they want, in this case away from kids when they want.

I think people in groups will want kids of their own less because their needs for involvement with them are already largely filled. They've been involved with them in the group or groups they've lived in, as children themselves, and as older kids and adults looking after and interacting with kids (hopefully, only when they've wanted to). If new kids have somehow been joining a group, its kid population hasn't grown older together the way it would in a nuclear family. So group members have stayed involved with kids since they were kids themselves.

And I think people who have a child in a group or bring one into it will want less to have another to keep the first one company. Less than in the isolation of a nuclear family. If I were a parent, I'd try to pick or organize a group with kids about the same age as mine.

And I have the feeling that adults living in a group won't want the adult:kid ratio to get much below 2:1. Down toward 1:1, things could get out of hand. Oo-oo. Group's going to determine how many kids in the group, which could translate to *who* gets to have kids: do what you want, except what the group *doesn't* want. Frankly, I don't think it would take the whole group or even much of it to have that dampening effect. If I thought my group were saturated with kids, I'd say so on the wants/needs board. I certainly plan to say so if there aren't enough of them. If a few others posted the same thing, I'd think someone wanting a child would try to find or organize a group where the child would be more welcome. Ask for what you want, give what you want to give, and see what happens.

Or scream and carry on. I want a baby and I want it *here*. Maybe if everybody screams and carries on, a lovely solution will evolve that everybody totally supports. It's my untested faith that things like this happen in an emotional work context.

"I don't need my own kid, I'm involved with plenty of them already," "my kid certainly doesn't need any more company than he/she's already got," and "let's not let our adult:kid ratio get out of hand": I think these population demotivators will emerge spontaneously—and powerfully—if the kind of group living I'm describing catches on. And these demotivators will skew human population downward. Downward more: growth rates are already dropping, as we've seen.

I think group living rooted in emotional work will also be *the* vehicle for massive declines in human consumption. People living in groups of this kind will consume less because they're fulfilling their fundamental needs more.

SEX

INTIMACY

NURTURING

FAMILY

BODY ACTION

MIND ACTION

LOVE

FEELINGS

These are the needs I've proposed as fundamental. And meeting them is what the group living I've been describing is all about. Except for sex. We haven't put that in yet. But all the others, the whole description above of group living is a description of meeting these fundamental needs.

I'm going into the Woods Place to do and get what I want and need most. Maximum fun, maximum fulfillment. And to experience feelings that come up along the way. And one of the most fun, fulfilling things I'll do is get behind others doing all this, who, I think, once they get into the fun of it all, will do it to each other. Again, humanity-consuming chain reaction contagion. Emotional work.

Now I think some who drift into the Woods Place and get involved in emotional work are going to hang around. I mean, nobody's chasing them off. They're only telling them to do what they want, which, in at least some cases you'd think, would be to hang around.

Not that I'd be above telling someone who's taking a lot more energy from the setup than he's reciprocating, or who for some other reason I don't like, that I want him to leave. I might even urge others to tell him the same thing. And of course, others are free to do this: tell someone they want him to leave and urge others to tell him too. We're all here to get what we want most. I like to think that only infractions of this order—taking a lot more than giving—would motivate expulsion. I like to think the dynamics of emotional work, including the wants/needs board, will resolve matters before they get to this.

So anyway, maybe some who want to hang around will want to put up dwellings. Nobody's stopping them. I expect to support them—say so on the wants/needs board, say yes if they ask, or just tell individuals I want them to.

I'm not yet ready to give away something as valuable as this land, so I may require agreements that no one gains any title to it by simply living on it. You want to own a piece or share ownership of it all so you can feel fully involved: right on. No doubt the less the Woods Place is mine the more it'll work. But make it less mine by just giving it away, I don't know. Maybe.

Emotional work, people hanging around, dwellings: a group living environment is springing out of emotional work. I assume at least *one* of the reasons people are hanging around and building dwellings is the emotional work in the air, the support, the feelings, the get-it-all, the fun of giving. It's attractive, isn't it, an environment whose very nature is fulfillment of wants and needs?

But why group living? Why can't people just drift in and out of *any* place where people are doing emotional work without living there? They can, and I hope they will. I hope they'll drift in and out of ones people live in and ones they don't. I want to see EW rooms in cities: soundproofed, mattresses, pillows, where you can go day or night and blow out or otherwise experience feelings and find others for mutual support. Free therapy—all of us need it. I want to see EW rooms in the work place.

So why group living? Why add that? One need you presumably won't fulfill in the come-and-go places is family. You might get a nice family feeling if most of the same people use the same EW place regularly. I think you'll get more of the feeling if the place happens to be where you and others live.

A deeply fulfilling coziness with others, that's my perception of family. A coziness we all need badly and customarily pass off as frivolity or take for granted at paltry levels. One particularly important application is kids sleeping with other kids, their parents, other adults, when they want, which may be always. If you don't want to sleep with kids, then don't. And if they don't want to sleep with you or anyone else, then for God's sake don't try in any way to get them to. But I think an environment like this will make it easier for kids, for everybody, to sleep with other people, or just be around them, cozy with them when they want.

Kids are ultimately what will draw people to live in EW groups most of the time, I'm convinced. Though I subgrouped kids under family, the need for them, I think, is primal. Right up there with sex. We—females *and* males—need to have them, bear them, raise them. Even if we don't do all these, we need to be involved with them some portion of the time for some portion of our lives. Kids are what family is all about. Always have been, always will be.

And I think people will conclude that EW groups are the best place to fulfill these kids-related needs. All those practical pluses: pooling time, energy and money providing food and cleaning up after it, pooling other responsibility for kids, providing much more freedom for parents, without baby sitters and day care. And finally, the much higher levels of safety in group living.

The need to be alone is as primal, I think, as the need to be involved with kids, particularly when you *are* involved with them. I'm convinced group living will enable parents to be alone a lot more than the nuclear family does today. Without forcing kids to take naps and otherwise sleep or disappear when they don't want to. I think people will conclude that EW groups are the best place for kids to grow up. The kids'll conclude it. Listen to them.

A big assumption is that experiencing feelings totally, slamming them out in groups for instance, will work as well as I think it will in resolving the problems that proliferate among people living together. Problems that make you prefer the torch—self-incineration—to living that way.

Sex and ego. Two huge and no doubt related drives that will muck up group living pretty thoroughly, don't you think? They always have. By ego drive, I mean the desire to be better than others, to win the competition that permeates all life everywhere, the drive for the mind/body rush of being hot and glad of it, hotter and gladder than anyone else.

I'm convinced that ego drives us to do most of what we do, more even than sex does. Why am I writing this book? To save humanity. Apocalypse-class ego rush, wouldn't you say? Call me a fool, but that motive has driven this book.

To be honest, I have no idea whether sex and ego will mess up EW group living. I want to try it, and if anybody else does, sex and ego will come up, any argument there? My faith remains what it's been throughout: fill yourself up, do, get it all. Fulfill our sex and ego needs and we'll consume less. And we'll compete less. We'll become our life system's first non-competitive species. Or radically *less* competitive species. The ultimate payoff of the climax of technology. Which is why the climax of technology is the climax of life, of evolution.

I'm writing this book to sell emotional work, not group living. My deepest conviction is that emotional work, by radically increasing fulfillment of human needs, will contribute to radical drops in human consumption. But I think most of us will be living most of the time in EW groups when declines in human consumption really kick in. And the group living will make the emotional work stronger and more effective. I think EW group living will enable humans to reduce or avoid altogether the kind of economic and emotional catastrophe that radical drops in consumption would otherwise entail. It will enable us to make a consumption soft-landing.

And we'll be living in EW groups because that's where we'll want most to be living. Not because they're the good, right, noble, the Earth-sparing and humanity-saving way to live. We'll live in them because they're the most fun, fulfilling, sexy and productive way to live. When they're not, we'll be living somewhere, some way, else. But for most of us, most of the time—EW groups, I think. What the Woods becomes, I hope.

What If We Did?

Recap. Advancing technology increasingly requires four things of the culture making it which keep culture members from fulfilling fundamental needs. Culture members can survive and indeed flourish without fulfilling these needs. Sex, for example, is fundamental, any argument there? Any argument that hosts of humans have survived without fulfilling it? Here are the four again:

SOCIAL COOPERATION
POPULATION GROWTH
CONSUMPTION GROWTH
GROWING HIERARCHIES

But at its climax, technology reverses its requirements, threatening the continued survival of the tech culture unless members start doing what the climax frees them to do—fulfill those fundamental needs. If they don't, their consumption continues to accelerate, and this in turn accelerates both their competition with other species, wiping out those that don't contribute in some way to their nourishment, and their competition with other tech species members, resulting in nuclear war.

I've argued that on Earth, the climax has started. Hierarchy growth has started to turn around, reducing restraints on sex, love, physical nurturing and emotional intimacy. And population growth has also started to reverse, which should free us to have sex with ourselves, people of the same sex, and close relatives. Hmm.

Perhaps it's time to address the central what-if question of the essay. Fill yourself up. Do, get all you want and need most. What if you did? Steal, rape, kill, molest, toddle on the freeway, drugs, suicide, fraud, hurt others physically and emotionally, persecute minorities, cheat on wife, sex with Mom, Dad, Junior, Sis, amuse yourself by abusing yourself all day every day, every kind of sex with whatever, get AIDS, die. And consume: buy buy buy, gobble gobble gobble. Do what you want. Do nothing: vegetate.

First off, my supporting your doing and getting what you want and need most doesn't mean that others are going to let you. This book is not an exhortation to abolish laws. Many will disappear in time, I hope. I think laws generally will become irrelevant in time. We won't need them.

But here, now, I can't take the environment away. In fact, I expect to contribute to the part of the environment that tries to prevent a lot of this stuff. I plan to put on the wants/needs board that I want everybody to obey all laws, even ones I don't like, that I will report violations I find out about and otherwise cooperate with law enforcers, and that I want others to do the same (I can't make them, of course). So far as possible, I want the law on the Woods Place's side, since neighbors, at least initially, might not be.

Judas. Scab. Hypocrite. You just tubed the whole thrust of the book. Do what you want while I call the cops. Slick front cover sucked me through every page of this gyp!

No it didn't. No I'm not.

As I say, getting behind people doing and getting what they want and need most is an intense turn-on for me. Kids, for instance. You want to climb a tree. If I'm scared, I'll take care of *me*. I'll do whatever I can to minimize danger to you without inhibiting your doing what you want. After all, something happening to you would be about the worst thing that could happen to me.

The real turn-on is to see what you do up in the tree, and I've seen enough of this to consider it a safe bet. The care with which you manage the tree. You're scared. I don't have to be scared for you (*"Becarefulbecarefulbecareful!!"*). You're out at the threshold between what you can do and what you want to be able to do—you're evaluating, theorizing, testing, reaching forward, stepping back.

You're an organism. Organisms equals feelings. And keeping you alive is what your feelings are about. Alive in both senses: away from death *and* hungry for life, for growing and expanding, hungry for fun.

But, again, I can't take the environment away. And I don't see an environment evolving in which people don't resist—resist collectively—being hurt by others, having things they consider their own taken from them, being forced to do things they don't want to do. I *do* see an environment evolving where people no longer want to do stuff like this to each other.

Steal, rape, kill, cheat, hate, persecute, manipulate. Don't do it. If I get the opportunity, I might try to stop you. You'll hurt yourself too much, I think. You won't fulfill fundamental needs and you'll lose power to fulfill those needs. You lose power when you're hiding from the law, when you're in prison, or dead.

Even if you don't get caught, you lose. It hurts to hurt others. I've done it, and I hurt. And the only way to harden yourself against the hurt is to suppress feelings. And suppressing feelings is a crummy way to live. We don't have to live that way anymore, I think.

For those of you who feel gypped that I might support the cops arresting you as much as you doing what they're arresting you for, maybe there's this consolation: no matter what feeling motivates what action, I'm for it—the feeling. "I want to kill the bitch. I want to *rape* her to death." "I want every penny of that cocksucker's." Scream it, slam it, process it in silence, I *totally* support the wanting. They can't arrest you for that.

People who deeply experience feelings that ordinarily motivate acts like the above don't commit them. Experience away the feeling—which I'm convinced is what happens to experienced feelings, they go away—experience it away and where's the motivation for the act? Gone. History. Assuming you're not seriously deprived of other fundamental needs. If you are, then the feeling and motivation might come back. Experiencing feelings is only one need I want us all to fill.

Does call-the-cops apply to all those do/get-it-alls above? What about suicide, drugs, toddling on the freeway, i.e. do what you want most, toddler, and take the consequences? What about all those nasty forms of sex: masturbation, pornography, promiscuity, homosexuality, incest, pedophilia? And consumption? What about that? 911? All of them?

In ten or so years of supporting people finding their own paths and taking them, I've never found myself supporting murder, theft or rape. They haven't come up. Anger, greed, lust? Oh yes, plenty of them. But not murder, theft or rape. Suicide's another story: it comes up routinely. It's up now.

Last night one of my closest friends told me she's decided "to go," as she puts it, "in a month, six weeks tops." Diagnosed a year ago as manic depressive, Edith has been hospitalized most of the time since. She has accumulated debts she believes she can never repay, she and her three successive psychiatrists believe her illness is biochemical and genetic, and they've tried a broad range of drug treatments with effects ranging from none to catastrophic. She's not particularly aware of ever having been manic, except that she's been extremely productive most of her life when not depressed. Now the depressions are too long and severe: if she's not in one, she feels one coming. She's always running when she's not caught. And she sees no relief. She has always, since she was a child, viewed death as positive, not just as relief from life. Living is like a joke, she says, that everybody else gets, but she doesn't. "Ultimately it's a matter of taste. You like brussels sprouts, I *don't* like brussels sprouts."

Edith is in her early 30s, great looking, she's had plenty of excitement, all kinds. And she wants, as she says, to go—responsibly, methodically, her things in order. Do what you want to do most?

What's the point of enduring a relentlessly painful life for which there appears to be no remedy? Want to go? I support it. I may not want to break the law over it, but generally I support it.

The problem is, Edith has demonstrated to my satisfaction an ability to make life rewarding for herself and for others *if* she can shake the depressions. And for that I don't think she's done all she can.

Joan Goldberg saw Edith once for the better part of a day. Joan and I would like to see her cold-turkey her drug intake: nicotine, well over a pack a day, caffeine, and prescription medications which in the last year have been aimed at depression, anxiety, severe back pain and diarrhea. The back pain and diarrhea were apparently side effects of the antidepressant and anti-anxiety drugs. During the five years I've known her Edith has taken prescriptions for skin rashes, warts, and other infections including at least one venereal disorder. Other than occasional alcohol, she does not use party drugs, though she did before I knew her.

Joan and I want her to drop milk--she drinks about two gallons a week. And we want her to get intensive reparenting/emotional work or other psychotherapy to deal with, for one thing, a history in adolescence of severe physical and emotional abuse by her father. Edith has had some therapy, but she never really gave in to it and tested its possibilities.

What am I supposed to do? What do I *want* to do? It's the very nature of what I want to happen to Edith that nobody but she can make it happen. Lock her up? Take away her cigarettes, medication and milk? Give her only fresh fruits and vegetables, grains and legumes and hope she eats them? How do I make her experience the feelings and meet the needs that I'm convinced are at the root of her depression? Only she knows what her feelings and needs are, and only she can feel and fill them. The timing is uncanny: I'm actually writing this in the middle of this crisis, so we'll have to wait to see the outcome.

Drugs. Just say no to drugs. What if you just feel yes to drugs? I love them. I love marijuana, LSD, tried freebase, coke, mushrooms. Grass was the one, 1967-82. Not that much, but enough. Some acid trips. The others I tried, but barely, and by the time I'd stopped grass, I'd stopped everything else.

What gives people the right to keep you from ingesting what makes you feel good? Even if it harms you? What gives people the right to stop you from harming yourself? Same thing that gives them any right: might.

"We have the right to vote," cried women and blacks in this century. If you have the right to vote, why aren't you voting? You're not voting because you *don't* have the right: you haven't exerted enough power to get what you seem to think you've already got. If you had the right to life, liberty and the pursuit of happiness, did you have to kill all those young redcoats just to make the point? You *didn't* have the right. You *weren't* born with it. Might is the basis of all rights. Give me an exception.

Why do people want to use their might to prevent you from harming yourself? Well, you represent a lot of investment—economic, emotional—and investors aren't going to recoup, economically or emotionally, if you're strung out on drugs or dead.

But oh the problems people create when they try to prevent others from getting what they want. Try to interfere with drug commerce by severely punishing the merchants and movers, and retail prices go into orbit, along with crime committed to meet the price, the cost of enforcing the law—which isn't enforced—and official corruption. The money gets crazy, along with what people do to get it. The drug frenzy.

One way or the other, it's the individual, I think, who has to come to his or her own terms with drugs, whether they're legal or not. My terms are that they're all bad: caffeine, nicotine, alcohol, party drugs. And I'm convinced that over-the-counter and prescription drugs are way over-used—for essentially the same reason illegal ones are.

I don't expect the law to let children use drugs. Nor does big money, killing, corruption and expensive "enforcement" have much to do with the 6-12 market. Or even the 18-and-under. It's adults. The statistical likelihood is that one in five of the 20- to 40-year-old men and women you see every day is using illegal drugs to some extent. The killing and corruption originates with these nice folks. They make the market and the price.

We certainly have no trouble letting people harm themselves enough ways. Deaths related to alcohol have been running around 100,000 a year in the U.S., nicotine around 350,000, and other drugs in the 3,500 range.

Legalize drugs. Let the prices, crime, corruption and cost to the taxpayer of law non-enforcement plummet. Let the frenzy fizzle, and let adults work out for themselves whether and to what extent they want to live. To me, the drug crisis is the culminating payoff of a culture that believes it's not good to fully process real feelings and to meet real needs. Experience your feelings, meet your needs, and you won't want to use drugs, that's my argument.

Kids. I love them. I love to follow toddlers and see what they do. And get behind their doing it. It seems to me parents spend a lot of time and energy reining them in, keeping them from doing what they want, making them do what they don't want. But if you don't restrict kids' actions, how do you get anything else done besides following them and getting behind what they want to do?

It's an ideal I'm proposing. A different one than, look how my kid minds, am I an authority figure or what? I see parents stop their kids from doing stuff just to show how good a parent they are. Or how bad they're not. How inspiring, a nation of unbad parents. Who not only slow kid down from moving his or her threshold out, from growing and expanding, but who also miss for themselves the experience I find so intense. Who make the whole child-rearing process so much more painful—for everybody—than it needs to be.

Right from the beginning, "Sh-sh baby, it's alright." If it's alright why is baby screaming? Why try to invalidate what baby is experiencing, which is that it's *not* alright? How about "Ye-es, it's terrible, isn't it?" Same tone of voice, while trying to correct whatever's wrong. *You* know something's wrong. If you don't think anything's wrong, why are you peeing your pants trying to figure out what's causing the screaming? "Yes, it's terrible" is just as natural, I think—much more so, in fact. That or "Yeah, really" or even "All the way. Total. Blow it out, Babe!" Get behind the kid. Behind what he/she is experiencing, and what he/she wants to do and get—while still trying to correct what's causing the screaming, of course. Surrender to self interest: who wants to listen to screaming? The result, I think, is fewer headaches and more growth for both.

I don't want to "feed" and "dress" kids. By that, I mean I don't want to decide when and what they ought to eat and wear and then make them do it. They're organisms. They know when they're cold and hungry, and when they are, they do something about it. Even a

newborn. Screaming, telling me what they want, that's doing something. And as I say, I like to give people what they want, not what I
think they ought to want.

A scenario I like and that I think could be representative *and* practical runs like this. I don't fix kid food (I'm talking toddler now, old
enough to be interested in food a male can supply). I don't even ask if
he/she wants any food, much less what. I fix *me* food. I sit, lie down
with it. Small person climbs up/squats down, studies food, tests it,
eats it all for all I care. Maybe I get some squirmy cuddles but no
food. There's more. Even if there isn't, who should get it? (I admit, if
a toddler's around, I just might use the blender more when making
my food.)

Small person eats when and what he/she wants. Cries, screams,
any way he/she communicates hunger, I try to give what they want
when they want it. That's the ideal. The child makes the decisions,
not me.

Same with clothes. Wear them when you want, which I'd imagine
would be when you need. Otherwise why bother? You go outside, it's
cold, *you* deal with it. Scream, tell me to get you what you want, or
get it yourself. Whichever.

I don't like insulating your response to your environment, making
you take protection before you know what you're protecting yourself
against. I think optimal safety and health dictate that *you* respond to
your environment and *you* decide what to do about it. I'll take care
of *me*. I'll be there to support what you decide, to take orders. I am
the Emperor. That's what post-Climax Emperors do. Take orders, give
power, and that way get all they want and need.

So what do you do when toddler toddles over toward the freeway?
Or does anything comparably dangerous? The ideal is that I take care
of myself and toddle toward freeway too, but that something about
the freeway, the noise, the size and speed of the vehicles, scares toddler

who turns and heads in the other direction. But of course I wouldn't be taking care of me if I didn't intend to act should toddler *not* turn and head the other way. I'm Spontaneous Me—my ultimate dogma for living. I get to do what *I* want, too. I get to pick toddler up and carry him/her to safety if I want.

As I say, it's an ideal, a course to steer as best *I* think is practical and makes *me* feel best. It makes *me* feel best when I can get behind kids doing what they want most of the time. When what they're doing doesn't make me feel best, when, for instance, it frightens me too much, I act. But I hate to act. I hate to decide for them and force them. Hence the motive for the ideal. An ideal I offer you for your greater pleasure and the betterment of our species.

And now, at long last: sex.

I love sex. I long for the day when we'll treat it—all of it, all that pleases all the organisms involved—with the same sober reverence we now accord God, country, alma mater. Always dirty jokes, laughter and fun, mind you. More, in fact. Dirty jokes, laughter and fun deserve supreme sober reverence. My sex history is particularly lame, so I'm particularly unqualified to make judgments about it, but I'm going to anyway. I already have.

First, the most culturally sensitive instance of sex: that involving children. Children are intensely sexual. I'm convinced of this by my own experience as a child, by my observations of children throughout my life, and by psychological and anthropological studies on the subject. It's all there: the energy, the intensity, the sexy desire to see, touch, feel, think, say, do. Kids are horny little angels—until you chew them out enough about it and they back off, feel guilty and inferior, "immature," and try to forget about it. I regard this coerced latency as the true loss of innocence, justifiably imposed by needs for sex control *prior* to the climax of technology.

In the best of all possible worlds soon to come, activity that we would now regard as sexual will occur among children and adolescents, it'll be fun and fulfilling and nothing else for everyone involved or else it won't happen, and everyone will be the healthier and more powerful for it. But a lot of things have to fall into place before that does.

We adults must first reach for all we want/need most, experience feelings that get in the way, and discover the fun of getting behind others doing the same. We must become an emotional work culture.

My conviction is that the more we let go of trying to guide children, steer them, manipulate them into directions our judgment dictates, the more we start turning responsibility for their lives over to them—right from the beginning—the more we simply support *their* judgment, then the more children are going to talk about, among other things, the sex that's going on in their consciousnesses and in their lives.

We're the ones who shut them up on the subject. We adults, and also child peers who have absorbed more of the culture's standards: "Gross" said a friend's boy, 8, to his 5-year-old brother who was fondling his genitals. "But it feels so goo-ood," responded Hero and Prophet of Post-Climax Humankind.

The more they talk about sex in their consciousnesses and experience, the safer kids are going to be from sexual things happening to them, *any things* happening to them, that they don't want to happen. Things other than what they want to happen most. They're going to be safer because you and others in their lives will know what's happening. Because they're telling you. You'll give them the support they want in avoiding things they don't want. And you'll support them in experiencing feelings stimulated by things they didn't want. No more lonely, secret mortification, indeed obliterated memory and seemingly rootless depression later in life, for being possibly to blame for what you hated. Or at least hate in retrospect.

At the same time, I think rape of any kind, getting anybody to do anything he/she doesn't want to do, will progressively disappear as emotional work culture emerges, as people become more adept at getting all they want and need most and as they turn on to getting behind others doing the same. Getting sex from someone who doesn't want to give it to you isn't what we want the most. It's something we'll settle for in desperation or anger if we're not satisfying stronger, deeper wants and needs.

The assumption is that those you're fulfilling yourself with are fulfilling themselves just as much with you. I don't think your fulfillment amounts to much if that's not the case. If you can put up with fulfilling yourself with someone who isn't doing so with you, the law *won't* put up with it. It never has and it never will. My argument is that in time it won't have to. We'll be good enough at securing the all-the-way fulfillment, in which everyone else involved is just as fulfilled, that the law will be irrelevant. The ultimate happily-ever-after. And we're heading for it, I believe.

Part Four
Seed

EDITH

Into the stretch, with first some bitter business.

My friend Edith destroyed herself as planned, connecting a vacuum cleaner hose from her car exhaust to her car window. Not long after telling me she planned to kill herself, she showed me the hose she was going to use, tucked cozily in her bedroom closet with the vacuum cleaner. Sure, I said to myself when she showed me the hose--I was fairly confidant then that something would turn things around and she wouldn't use it. Edith wanted as little pain as possible and concluded that carbon monoxide was her best shot. I hope she was right.

Edith had cut me out of her life by the time she killed herself because I had joined a suicide intervention effort a month before. Someone had warned me that trying to intervene would likely end the relationship. It did.

I had joined the intervention at the last minute. There were four of us: an ex-lover of Edith's, a woman friend of his, one of Edith's sisters, and me. I joined after hearing the argument of a manic depressive who led support groups for other manic depressives. The suicide intent, he insisted, stemmed from Edith's illness—also called bipolar disorder. The intent should be blocked at all costs so the right medication or combination of them could be found to control the disorder with a minimum of side effects.

Edith had been prescribed a lot of drugs and combinations of them, and she had dived into each new regimen with the desperate conviction that this would be the one. But for all the regimens she and her succession of psychiatrists tried, it's unlikely they had exhausted all possibilities for pharmacological relief.

More than a week before I joined the intervention group, one member had contacted the state's Crisis Intervention unit, the agency charged with suicide prevention. I was in close touch with the interveners but wanted to delay calling in outside authorities. Edith had made her thoughts clear about that idea.

It was never hard to convince anyone of Edith's intentions: she had terminated her apartment lease without looking for another place to live, and she was giving away her possessions. She gave me the better part of her large and excellent collection of rock LPs. I accepted it to buy time: we spent an afternoon going through it, arguing who was good and who wasn't. She was nuts about Elvis Costello. She had gone to a concert in Philadelphia the previous year and Elvis had picked her from the audience to dance on the stage. She danced her ass off and loved it.

The Crisis Intervention people wanted to move quickly, to visit her and try to persuade her to get back into some kind of treatment. Obviously, if she killed herself, they didn't want to have to explain why they had known of her intention for a week and done nothing about it.

I didn't want authorities to intervene because, for one thing, Edith, having made her suicide decision, felt great for the first time in at least a year. She busily and carefully divided up her collection of personal photographs and gave them to the people appearing in them. The ones I got were of me at her place the previous fall preening in a tuxedo on my way to a fancy-dress affair, and me with her dog when I brought him for a visit at the National Institute of Mental Health in Maryland where she spent the previous winter.

Cheerfully busy as she was, it didn't look like Edith was going to jump the gun. We were less than two weeks into her "one month, six weeks tops," and I thought maybe her friends could accomplish something before bringing in the authorities and making it a full-blown crisis. We couldn't do much *after* bringing in the authorities, I believed, and that certainly proved true.

Crisis Intervention asked members of the intervention group to have Edith call Crisis Intervention. Of course she didn't. At this point I was still dealing with Edith with the same scrupulous honesty I always had. As a result, when we talked over the phone about Crisis Intervention and she said there was something I wasn't telling her, I told her what it was: if she admitted Crisis Intervention to her apartment, they could seize her and commit her involuntarily.

So it was no surprise that when I joined the intervention and the four of us and two women from the Crisis Intervention unit met outside her apartment door and knocked, we got no answer. It was a sweltering and humid Friday of Fourth of July weekend. Edith lived on the second floor of a once-grand building shaded by ancient, venerable trees. But the shade did little this day.

We were sure she was inside because I had called and, for the first time ever, lied to her and said I was just checking in to see how she was. Now we shouted and knocked on her front door inside the apartment building and on her kitchen door at the top of a long fire-escape stairway. But no response.

Her car was there, but here was an irony: after I got home from the intervention the following day--she was locked up in the state hospital by this time--there was a message on my answering machine. Edith: I've gone with my girlfriend to the beach for the weekend. The message might have muddied the waters had we gotten it in time.

I tried to woo her with humor by hollering in that I'd brought two dozen sushis from her favorite sushi bar. Sushi ranked with sex as a core passion in Edith. She only stopped eating it, she said, when she either ran out of money or decided she was stretching somebody's generosity too thin. She got me for about fifty bucks' worth one night. But the sushi routine on this occasion accomplished nothing.

Crisis Intervention could not force entry, so after an hour the Crisis Intervention women left. They suggested we contact the police, an option we felt we had to take because of the possibility, however remote, that, since her closest friends had shown their hand, Edith might now be doing what we were all trying to prevent. One of us stayed behind so we would know if she left.

The police intervention was by nature an atrocity, though the men who executed it were, I feel, entirely professional and decent. We had a long wait at the Wilmington police station before two young officers were assigned to us, and more time while we drove to a hospital to get a psychiatrist's authorization for forced entry.

When we all arrived back at Edith's, there was still no response when we knocked. The two officers were shortly joined by a third, older and higher ranking. The officers spent half an hour trying to get Edith to open the kitchen door that was up the long fire escape stairway. This time we interveners stayed nearby but out of the picture. It was night and the police presence made for a much more serious, indeed sinister atmosphere. Only the officers called for Edith now.

I was a little way from the back of the house and close enough to watch the lead officer at the door. He finally gave up trying to contact Edith and, in short but fierce movements, heaved his shoulder twice against her door, ripping away the door frame on the lock side. He then unclipped his holster, drew his gun, held it up next to his shoulder just like in the movies, and moved cautiously into Edith's dark kitchen.

From outside I heard him summon the other officers. They followed him in. Shortly after, one of the young officers signaled us to come in, which we did. I was the first of the amateurs to cross through the kitchen and enter the main room. Edith was lotused on her bed, smoking, a book in her hand. She was dressed in skimpy white shorts and pink tank top. Her long blond hair was tied up to beat the heat. When she saw me, she pointed straight at me and bellowed "And *you*. Get the *fuck* out of here!"

"Just a moment, Edith," the lead officer said, taking the gentle-but-firm tack. "This might be your apartment, but right now we're in charge. We decide what goes on here, understand?" She didn't argue.

He then continued a line of questioning he'd already started. "So you have no intention of committing suicide, is that what you're saying?"

"That's right," chirped Edith, smiling cheerfully.

"But you've terminated your lease on this apartment without getting another place."

"I'm going to live with a friend."

"Who?"

"I'd rather not say."

"I see. And I understand you're giving away all your possessions."

Edith gestured at the room full of furniture and possessions she still had. She then added, pointedly not looking at those of us who had received much of what she had given, "I guess *some people* just don't appreciate a little generosity."

The officer then asked us whether Edith had stated her intention to kill herself within six weeks. We said she had.

He then unclipped his pair of handcuffs—the real things looked much shinier and heavier than what I'd seen in movies or anywhere else. He said "Sorry, regulations require these," and asked Edith to put her hands behind her back. She did, easily sustaining her cheerful, fuck-you eagerness to cooperate.

The officer then asked Edith where her apartment keys were. Enraged at me as she was, Edith still let me take her keys from the front pocket of her skimpy, tight shorts. She even jutted her hip my way sarcastically as if to help.

Because Edith refused to be hospitalized voluntarily, she couldn't go to a private facility and was taken instead to Delaware State Hospital outside Wilmington. I'm told it's not one of your cheerier state mental hospitals, and that jibed with what I saw.

I last saw Edith when I took cigarettes to her late that same night at the hospital. She ordered them like a dragon when she called her apartment and learned it was I who guarded it and her dog, since her forced door now didn't. Edith sat in the lobby of her locked ward in a pink, full-length nightgown, wrapper and slippers, all hospital issue. She looked rather grand and Jean Harlow in her floor-length, dingy pink, but it was a grandeur entirely out of character with her own. In the five and a half years I knew Edith I saw her in a dress only once, bright red and quite flouncy, in a videotape of a broth-er's wedding. When I brought the cigarettes, she neither spoke nor looked at me, so I gave them to the attendant at the nurse's station and left.

I spoke to her by phone twice during her ten-day confinement. Each call was about care for her dog which I had with me. She hat-ed that I had her dog but couldn't do much about it. Intermediaries urged me otherwise not to contact her.

Prior to this, Edith and I had exchanged barely an unkind word in all the years we knew each other. She felt entirely betrayed by me. She had probed me laboriously on the subject of suicide, and I had chimed in dependably with my support litany, aimed at the desire, not the act—though I probably made that clear only after she announced her decision.

It didn't bother me at that point not to see Edith for a while. I felt burned-out from at least a year of her mental health crisis. And frankly Edith scared me. She could be vindictive—she had stories to support this claim—and who could say *how* vindictive if she had nothing to lose.

During her confinement I drafted a letter that I wanted to reach whomever got primary responsibility for Edith. I went over the letter with friends and family members actively involved in the whole crisis, spelling out why we felt Edith was a danger to herself and should be watched closely.

In a short time, she accepted a new psychiatrist and voluntarily entered a private facility. Edith got her new psychiatrist with the help of a friend who had not been involved with the intervention. I was concerned that if Edith knew the psychiatrist had gotten the letter, particularly if I were its source, she wouldn't work with this psychiatrist. So I tried to get the letter to him via another friend who had not been involved in the intervention.

I don't think the letter ever reached the psychiatrist, so I'm not sure he knew how serious Edith was about her suicide intention. Obviously, she wasn't about to enlighten him. Anyway, about ten days after the intervention, Edith was released and free to put the vacuum cleaner hose to use, which, in about three weeks, she did.

Why? Why did Mr. Do/Get-It-All try to stop Edith from getting what she clearly wanted most—maybe needed most? Why did I rupture a seamless relationship during her terminal crisis when she needed more, not less, support from those closest to her?

To cover my ass, for one thing. Edith had dropped her most recent psychiatrist and his associate psychologist after she'd told them of her suicide intention and they had said they might intervene. That left me as her principal confidant and source of emotional support. There were others, but not many. In any case, I felt I was left holding the bag as substitute shrink, and I felt I'd be playing God, at least in the eyes of others, if I simply urged Edith to do and get what she wanted most. Those are my values, not my culture's, and my culture's values have survived a lot more testing than mine have. And the opinions of others, then and later, on how I had managed in this situation counted to me. They still do.

Also, I was moved at the last minute by the argument of the support group leader: keep her alive so she can find some kind of tolerable drug combination that can relieve the depressions. I'll always worry that I did Edith harm by sharing my skepticism on drug therapy and the good I didn't think it would do her. I may have contributed to her quitting early the search she had set out on with such desperate conviction. Had she found some tolerable drug therapy, she might later have tried the things Joan Goldberg and I believe heal more completely.

Finally, I joined the intervention because I didn't want Edith to do and get what she wanted most any more than I want toddler to toddle the freeway. I can imagine supporting someone surrendering to what's happening to them when what's happening is they're dying. But Edith was young and strong. She had served in the merchant marine, and she loved to beat men at arm-wrestling in bars. She had a trick, I think, but boy, was it humiliating.

Vulgar, exciting and proud, she was loaded with the contradictions that make for being human. A particularly alive human. One of my favorite lines of hers came when she was reading a new resumé I had put together: "A quarter of the way down and I'm already wet." Handy with the compliment, that Edith.

She was in a bar with a bunch of girlfriends once when some guy came up, chatted genially and eventually started strutting his studly prowess, his skills and successes. In front of a little crowd that had developed Edith unzipped the guy's pants, pulled out his penis and announced, "Nah, not so great."

Edith had always wanted a baby, partly, no doubt, for the same reason most women do, but also, I think, in the hope that pregnancy and motherhood would chase away the blues. She became pregnant about six months before the depression crisis started but miscarried within a few weeks.

Soon after the miscarriage, Edith and her boyfriend went to Rio for Carnival. She'd only been out of the country once, to Europe some ten years before. She loved the carnival cult of virtual nudity, the lasciviousness, the contests and floats, but the highlight of the trip was flying down one of the mountains bordering the city on the back of a professional hang-glider.

Not long after getting back from Rio Edith single-handedly organized a campaign against some injustice at the main Wilmington, Delaware postal facility where she worked. The climaxing march and rally drew support from Delaware's governor, its one U.S. representative and both senators. Not surprisingly, the campaign was successful, but Edith collapsed immediately afterwards, beginning the terrible year before her death.

To me, Edith was equipped to have a dynamite life. Obviously, she'd had moments, plenty of them. And I balked at her throwing away what I considered her one shot for more, longer and better moments.

I don't believe in God. I don't believe he's up there, in here or wherever. There are powers and forces inside and outside me that are plenty bigger than my imagination, will or strength. You want to call these powers and forces God? Okay. But when you identify them as God, you haven't yet included capabilities that people most want God to have. You haven't included, for example, the ability to respond to worship and prayer. Dear God, get me out of this mess, make me feel good, make the phone ring, make my life better, deliver me, deliver my people. I don't believe there's an agency that can respond to such appeals.

I don't believe there's any agency that guides the comings and goings of the universe and distinguishes between good and evil and punishes one and rewards the other. I don't believe there's any agency that's somehow looking out for me and knows my destiny. I don't believe in destiny. I believe that logic determines every event in the universe, logic that, once it's understood, can be seen as permitting little alternative. Destiny, yes, but not of the "some enchanted evening," "it is written" sort.

I don't believe in former lives, future lives, I don't believe I chose the circumstances I was born into, I don't believe I came into this life with a purpose, I don't believe things were meant to be. I believe, once you're dead, you and your consciousness are over. History. The molecular activity that energized your consciousness is doing other things, as it was before you were conceived. I believe the one and only consciousness that I'm inside never existed before my current life and won't exist after it. All the consciousnesses that existed before and after were and will be somebody else, not me.

How can I live without faith? This *is* my faith. Part of it. I think it's a beautiful part—one, for example, that doesn't divert love anywhere but where it's best served and from which it's best rewarded: me, other organisms, and everything else I can more or less see or touch in the universe. I love us. Hopefully some of us love me.

The miracle of life, of consciousness, me. And not just me: me *human*, me human *today*, at this advanced, possibly climactic stage of technological development. At this relatively lucky rank and status among humans. And the enormous power that all these advantages cumulatively afford—power to learn, experience, build and enjoy. Again, look back, look down the upward-curving evolutionary pyramid, the steadily steeper accumulation of advances that mark where you are. It stupefies me when I think how lucky I am. Almost makes me believe in God!

Do and get all you want and need most, but don't throw away all your ability to want, need, do or get anything. Don't make me support that. Particularly if you're young, strong and beautiful.

Well, Edith had every reason to believe she'd slid far down the pyramid and to feel less stupefied at her luck than I do. She faced a tidal wave of practical problems in the year after she first told me about her depressions. She stopped work. No savings, limited insurance protection, limited ability and willingness of friends to fill in. Rent, car payments, car insurance payments, prescriptions, food. I could have given everything I had, I felt at the time, and it wouldn't have been enough. I marked limits early on, mostly in the interests of the book, interests she quite sincerely endorsed. (If this book never makes it, I'll always have Edith's words for solace: that her neck got sore nodding in agreement.)

Oh yes, after she had decided on suicide, I offered the ranch, asked her to live at my place, I'd do everything, she could have the bedroom, which I barely used. "You're so cute" was her entirely sincere response. I wasn't offering what she wanted.

Closing irony: she had scrawled "Invalid—suicide" on her life insurance policy which named, among others, me. One of the others filed a claim for us and in a remarkably short time we each got checks for eighteen grand. Had she known the policy was valid—it was just over a year old, otherwise it wouldn't have been—I'm sure she would have changed at least one of the beneficiaries, a kind of detail Edith rarely missed. Another irony: the intervention delayed her timetable. Had she been able to act earlier, the policy might not have been valid. It was that close.

She's gone and I'm moving on. I wish I'd been able and willing to do more. Edith was immensely capable of fun, and I'm convinced many would have been enriched had she had more of it. I'm afraid we'll have to be satisfied with what we got.

Wrap-up

So. If population growth and hierarchy growth reverse, we should all be freer to fulfill needs which these two characteristics of technological culture suppressed. Sex, for instance: if you no longer want your population to grow, you don't have to block sex with yourself, others of your own sex or those too closely related to you. And indeed some of these taboos seem to be disappearing.

Masturbation for instance. Don't I hear authorities today *pressing* masturbation on young people as an alternative to intercourse and its dangers of pregnancy and communicable diseases? Masturbation that used to make us blind and crazy? (It kind of did make me blind and crazy.) Anyway, looks like we're putting that one well behind us, not a second too soon in my book.

Homosexuality. We were making some progress there before AIDS came along. You're an organism: learn precisely what to do to avoid AIDS and do it. Abandoning optimal sexual fulfillment is not what's required, I think.

Besides, AIDS isn't what our homo-thing is about. It just gave our homo-thing some muscle. "See? See what that gay stuff can do to you?" Get your feelings out about homos, about the stuff they do and—here it is—the *man* you ain't if you "are one" and "do that shit."

Manhood, virility: identity crap. Who/what are you? A cult of heterosexuality, revitalized by the AIDS disaster, permeates American culture. And I think it dehumanizes us. It makes us into identities, identities we sculpt and covet in terror and suspicion, suffocating authentic spirit no matter where that spirit would lust were it free. You want to be an identity, be my guest. I don't. I want to be an organism, and what this organism wants is to fulfill its authentic sexual, love and other here-now needs whatever they happen to be. And to get behind other organisms doing precisely the same.

So I'm proposing an alternative cult. Certainly not a homosexuality or pansexuality cult. A do/get what you want/need most *now* cult. Celibacy Lib, if it's what you want most. I support it totally.

Me Me Me. Now Now Now. The ideal, the perfection, toward which the cult constantly reaches. Reach there and you'll consume less and give more, that's my creed.

Incest. One of the major occurrences of the last ten or so years has been the awareness explosion regarding incest and child abuse and how much damage both have inflicted on how many lives. My only criticism of this awakening is its nearly-exclusive focus on sex.

The supreme horror encompassed by the term 'incest' is something happening to a child in the child's last refuge, the home, at the hands of possibly the last person to whom the child can look for protection: a parent, an adult relative, any trusted adult in that refuge. How vivid the meaning of "insecurity" becomes in such a context: so much so it's hard to believe that the horrific effects of incest don't occur in all instances of it. Maybe they do.

There are two great villains, I believe, in the devastating stories we've been hearing in recent years. The first is coercion in any form however subtle—getting people to do what they don't want to do. The second is our cultural environment which stigmatizes so many activities identified with sex as inherently evil, sick and destructive.

How do we deal with these villains? Here's my answer: do and get all you want and need most and experience the feelings that come up along the way. Don't violate the law. The penalty, even if you're not caught, is not what you want and need most. Become adept at meeting your needs and you'll never want to get anything from anyone who doesn't want to give it to you as badly as you want to get it. You'll never be a coercer/manipulator that way, because that's never what anybody wants the most. They'll accept it only as a meager substitute.

Also, reach for your deepest wants and needs and maybe you'll acquire a taste for getting behind others doing the same. And if you like that experience—seeing others meet all their deepest wants and needs—you can't be a contributor to the opprobrium that infects the vast range of human sexual drives, or resist the healing, strengthening and growth-promoting ways of fulfilling them.

Sex is fun, at least it should be. The best fun there is. I believe that adults who are used to getting what they want and need most will not want to fulfill their sex needs with people too young to reproduce. To the extent they do, the law and the collective conscience at the root of the law will act, as they do now and always should, to protect what they view as the interests of the child.

Here's what *I* view as the interests of the child. Children will only probe so far in their sexual curiosity. Being free to probe as far as they want *and no further*, getting support from others for probing as far as they want *and no further*, will make for healthy, powerful humans. And humans like this are what it's going to take to get us past the horrific dangers we face: such humans will be sexually free and sexually-fulfilled, and because of it, they'll consume less and give more—radically so.

Two of four characteristics of technological culture have started to reverse and thus allow us to meet more of our deepest wants and needs. But what about the other two: consumption growth and social cooperation? Are they reversing? Do they need to? Do we want them to?

Consumption is different from the other three characteristics: the others each contribute to the problem we're discussing by blocking human needs. But consumption doesn't have to block human needs to be a problem. It *is* the problem. Exploding human consumption today *is* eco-ravage and the threat of nuclear war. Reversing it is what this book is about. And reversing is by no means what consumption is doing.

But I've argued that while the consumption imperative doesn't directly block fulfillment of any fundamental human needs, it *helps* interfere with needs for family and for emotional intimacy. It helps us put distance between ourselves and other people—walls, lawns, lovely landscaping, suburban sprawl, cars. And affluent consumption enables us to be autonomous. We buy and own everything we want so we don't need others to help us meet our material wants and needs. We don't have to, yuck, *share*.

Consumption doesn't force us to distance ourselves from each other. It's just that, given our inclination to do so, it gives us the means. We want as little contact as possible, even within families, *particularly* within families in many cases. Contact generates feelings. And an archaic ethos still tells us it's bad to experience feelings.

I argue that when we experience our feelings more—much more, much more loudly maybe, violently even (not hurting anyone or anything)—we'll find we don't want all that distance from others, all that autonomy. So let go of the ethos of feelings suppression and we'll consume less—at least less of the stuff we put between each other.

Which brings us finally to social cooperation, the phenomenon in nature that makes us trembly-lipped, that moves us so deeply when we see it in the wild, if only *we* could be as cooperative as all those nice wild animals. Social cooperation is a technological imperative we *don't* want to reverse, right?

My problem with social cooperation is that it implies so much obligation. Do it because it's good and right, "correct," as they're saying today. Social cooperation involves sacrifice: I've argued it blocks all but one of the fundamental needs.

I think something much better is going to replace social cooperation. Emotional work culture. A culture that all humanity ultimately embraces. We'll embrace it because we, like all conceivable organisms in all conceivable universes, are selfish. Try that as the defining characteristic of life. If it's selfish, it's alive.

Emotional work culture: all of us doing and getting what we want and need most, fully experiencing the feelings that come up along the way, and—here's the stretch, the hypothesis upon whose extravagance a lot of this essay hangs—getting behind others doing the same. Getting behind them, again, not because it's good/right, save the planet, threatened species and all, but because it's fun, sexy, a turn-on, because it fulfills a fundamental human need. Maybe the ninth fundamental human need.

Giving. And the ultimate turn-on: giving precisely what recipient then and there wants most.

If we've always been selfish, why didn't our selfishness take this form? It did. We always gave. And we always loved it. Maybe all species do. We'll just give more. *Much* more. What we did a little bit will become the essential way human culture functions—including, I think, human economics, the generation and distribution of the goods and services humans want and need. We'll give our asses off, and we'll do it because we're selfish bastards.

But if giving has always fed some of our selfishness, why are we going to give so much more now than we used to? Because we can. The climax of technology allows us. It allows us to do what no species can do before their technology has climaxed: stop competing. Or at least compete much less.

Okay, how does *that* work? Soon technology will have delivered about all the safety and joy it can. At least the puberty growth spurt will be over. Adapting again and again to new onslaughts of technological change, each wave coming sooner and faster than the one before, all this will be a thing of the past—the experience, possibly, of a wistfully remembered heroic age (imagine: us, now, living in a heroic age!). And all the safety and joy technology will have finished providing will keep on doing what I maintain they've always done, again because of the logic of what technology is: spread to larger and larger portions of our species. Eventually all the joys and safety of technology will reach everyone.

But does this necessarily mean we won't compete anymore? It'll help. It'll mean nobody else will have access that you don't have to any of what technology has supplied. That ought to take some of the piss out of the frenzy.

We won't have to compete to stay alive. And we won't compete for material quality of survival since whatever we want materially will be generally as accessible to us as to anyone else. Inconceivable, isn't it? Absolutely unimaginable. But take a hard look at so many elements of our everyday lives today and how inconceivable and unimaginable they were only a short time ago. Personal computers? Even Flash Gordon and Captain Video didn't prepare us for them. Not even the *idea* of them.

Sex, love, non-material things, *ego*, will we compete for them? Maybe. But not on a scale, I think, that threatens nuclear war. Or charges the kind of frenzy that human competition is today.

Freed from at least much of the need to compete, people will do more, much more—here's the stretch again—of what the lucky ones always loved doing and everyone wanted to do more: give. Not before they've taken care of themselves, mind you. While, after, *maybe* before. That can be fun too.

Either way, Me First, always. Say what you like about this construct, it's built on the only principle that's ever made anything work: selfishness.

So. Competition*economics*, giving giving giving, *lusty* giving, Nirvana Utopia Heaven, *better than* Nirvana Utopia Heaven, with all this who needs social cooperation and all its sacrifices?

What if it doesn't all work out? What if the pieces don't fall together quite the way I'm saying they should? What if I guessed the logic wrong? What if logic has nothing to do with it? How much of this book would that invalidate?

A lot may hang on the book's central claim: if people fill their deepest animal needs—sex, intimacy, mind/body fun, and so on—their consumption will decline. Radically. On its own, without government, social or any other kind of intervention or pressure.

We consume as a replacement for fulfilling fundamental needs, instead of really getting off, cuddling down, really having fun, the kind of deep total fulfillment that consumption rarely supplies.

It's those sons-of-bitch old-time values, once essential to our survival, that still have a grip on us. Hero/martyr, back of hand to brow, I'll go without, *I'll* do the dishes. Deepest needs, what are they? Immature, dangerous, degenerate. Grow up, infant; back in line, deviant.

These values, critical to our coming far enough to need to leave them behind, run so deep, are cultivated in us so early, are so intrinsic to the cultural habit we pass on that we don't really know much about our deepest needs. We feel them, but we try to suppress them and feed them with consumption, we reward our self-deprivation with consumption. But consumption doesn't do it. So we consume some more, reward ourselves some more. In the past, great: the more we consumed, the more we advanced technology. Now the more we consume, the more we threaten everything.

Hey, I want more things. I want the land, the Woods Place, the dwellings, the AV entertainment center, I like music and movies (I want to share it all with other people). I want a camcorder, maybe some sports toys, new ski gear—I'll share them too. And I want to travel. Cheap. Mix it up with the locals.

Travel cheap, do cheap, live cheap. Step down. The supreme fun adventure the future holds for us. What we tried to do in the 60s, I think, but weren't quite ready for. Efficiency. What the human race needs more than it needs anything: radically better lives using radically fewer resources to live them.

If I thought everybody in the world were going to read this book the day it appeared (please do) and then immediately and drastically reduce their consumption, I'd be worried: overnight consumption crash is not recommended therapy for the world's current ills.

If what this book envisions comes to pass at all, it will start gradually and gather momentum. A few in the affluent ranges of the world hierarchy will taste emotional work a little, and if it works taste it a little more, and if it works more, others will see and taste it, and so on. The contagion. And the more the tasters taste, the closer they'll come to consuming less than they're producing, to stepping down.

If this process continues, affluent consumption growth will slow down, stop and reverse. It'll drop. Meanwhile consumption on the non-affluent side of the scale will continue what it's always done: rise. Only now it will rise faster as wealth from the inside is invested in or given more to the outside (as it always has been to some degree). Just because consumption is dropping in the affluent sector doesn't mean productivity is. And if affluent productivity remains stable or even grows, where's the spillover going to go? the only place it can: to the non-affluent sectors of the world.

Top comes down, bottom comes up. A flattening of consumption as part of a longer term consumption decline. In the meantime we'll be making technology, technology will be making technology, and its continued advancement at making itself more efficiently, making its products available for less, will help soften the impact of this flattening, of this consumption collapse.

We affluent humans want a lot of things. We want the starving people of the world to stop starving and start living normal lives like us. But God forbid human population should *grow*. We want to stop the cutting of the rainforests, the extermination of species, the polluting of the environment. And we want better living standards for ourselves. Not one of us wants to slide, not one least little bit. Better living standards for *everybody*. But no more war. Don't I see some conflicts here?

Help the starving people and you feed population explosion. Stop the rainforest demise and you help people starve. Ditto if you stop the extermination of species. Stop the pollution and you drive the cost of living up and your standard of living down, unless your income grows faster than the standard declines—in which case your consumption drives up rainforest destruction, species extermination, pollution of the environment, competition among humans and thus pressure for war.

A home of our own for every wholesome loyal American, but God forbid we should cut down pretty trees to build them with. Who do you think are going to be the next world champ consumers as marketization in the former Communist countries continues?

Freedom and democracy for everyone. One person, one vote. Whereby you can be sure places like the Serengeti Plain will be voted to corn, wheat, steers, or whatever the hell else people like eating more than they like eating lions and giraffes. And if world democracy really ran things, guess what would become of American immigration restrictions.

The soft spot in this knot, I think, is the human standard of living. The affluent human standard of living. Its decline will reduce the other pressures. It generates them.

Every human wants a better life for him/herself. Which for most of us most of the time means better *material* standard of living. And everything we do to achieve that standard of living aggravates the overwhelming problems it's the lot of the late 20th century and beyond to face. That we are facing these problems, trying to understand them, trying to act reasonably and effectively, maybe succeeding, maybe not, is why we're living in a genuinely heroic age. *The* heroic age, I believe.

Heroes of ancient Greece and the Golden West, the Gods of Olympus, the apostles and martyrs didn't face the prospect of blowing the planet to bits (most of them didn't know it was a planet) or consuming it to a sterile ball. They say we have no heroes anymore. Look around. *We're* facing all this.

No, if we've been facing it all the best we can, obviously our best hasn't been good enough. Yet. We have to do more. Go further. We have to go All The Way. Only this time, All The Way doesn't mean give up everything, sacrifice everything. It means *get* everything. Total greed, total surrender. Deep, inner, totally authentic Me Me Me. The

Emperor. A repellent idea, given our history, what always worked in it, and what we all came to believe as a result—what we *had* to believe for possibly millions of years. The enormity and completeness of this cultural flip is what makes it heroic. History's supreme heroic, I believe.

So there it is. The theory, the faith, the hypothesis. It's the way I think it'll work. The way I want it to work. The only thing I can do now is try it. Test the hypothesis, the faith. Go to the Woods Place, go for what I want/need most, experience the feelings that come up along the way, and do both *only* when and *only* because I want to. That's the ideal. Stay as close to the ideal as I can, be as purely selfish and greedy as possible, and from there the theory's on its own.

If it works, for kicks I'll look for opportunities to get behind others doing the same. And they in turn, in time, will look for like opportunities. And—if the theory works—the more we get of what we want and need most, the less we'll consume. The sublime contagion. The apocalyptic contagion.

Vote with your feet. You try your way, I'll try mine. If you have more fun, if you have a greater impact on the horrific dangers we face, or if it looks like you're surviving and I won't, I'll swing onto your path. Count on it. If I not only survive, but have more fun and maybe even an impact on the horrific dangers, maybe you'll swing onto the path I'm on. And if you don't, maybe your children will, or your grandchildren. Natural selection.

Start with little bites. Tiny steps. Tiny steps are heroic enough, selfish enough. Simon says take one tiny step, Simon says take one tiny step back. And this above all: *always* remember who Simon is.

I Am The Emperor

I was 12 when I first wanted to be Emperor. I discovered Napoleon in seventh grade history and I totally obsessed on him. It took more than one funny look to cure me of hand-in-shirt strut. War to me then was a huge game you won with dazzling strategy, and the spoils were *glory*. You, the conqueror in triumph, eight savage stallions drawing your chariot through the Arch of Titus, frenzied throngs teeming as far as the eye can reach, or behind the mounted *Garde Républicaine*, scarlet tassels bobbing from gleaming silver helmets against the backs of gleaming silver breastplates, through the Arc de Triomphe down the Champs Élysées, frenzied throngs teeming as far as the eye can reach: how do you *feel*?

"You dare to threaten the Emperor of the Universe." Charles Middleton trembling with rage as Ming in the Flash Gordon serials of the 30's and 40's, reducing me to jelly weekday afternoons in the 50's. Emperor of the Universe. Hard rank to top. Emperor of *all* universes? All times? All dimensions? Pretty close, there, to You Know Who.

Ego. What's it about? Where does it come from? From evolution, no doubt, but why? For the same reason any characteristic evolves: it makes those who have it more durable, more survivable than those who have less of it. Natural selection logic. If that's the case, if ego— and I'm using ego in the common parlance sense, "I'm the best," "watch this," not any psycho-technical sense—if evolution selected ego into us so we can out-survive those who have less of it or (gosh) none at all, why then do we sit on it so hard?

I love to see kids brag and show off. I love swelled heads. Trade you a stiff upper lip for one any day. Bragging and showing off equals growing, and crowing about growing, grabbing at acknowledgment for it. Praise. The sooner you get the acknowledgment and praise you need (*authentic* acknowledgment and praise, truly felt, the only kind that counts), the sooner you're off to grow some more. At any age.

Several times in Parks' groups I got up and stormed full-lung, sweating spitting stomping leaping, how great I am, how much I want, and I want it *ALL NOW. I* remember it as entirely authentic, no-baloney volcanic explosion, right from the core. It felt great, and the surprise was to see what it did to others. They stared up like kids looking at Santa Claus (ever been in a Santa Claus suit with young kids around? Christmas Eve when they expect the real thing? I did once, and I'll never forget it). Anyway, these ego-frenzy blowouts felt great to me, no surprise, but to those watching as well.

Am I unusually sick or unusually healthy? Am I unusual? Just what precisely are you Emperor *of*, Mr. Weymouth? Well, actually, not *of* anything. Emperor *for*. Emperor for all the states and all the nations and all the peoples and species of the Earth, EFASANAPSE. Well, that puts a cap on it. A trifle in Ming's realm, and way short of All Universes All Times All Dimensions (EAUATAD)—you're a colossus of modesty, Mr. Weymouth.

Yes, I think I'm unhealthy. Maybe unusually, I don't know. I'm way short of optimum, and one critical way I'm short is my desperate, seemingly limitless need for acceptance, for being important. Important to whom? To maybe everyone, at least to everyone who's important to me, and there have been many for whom I wasn't important enough. At least I didn't think I was. Maybe I was wrong. It doesn't matter, the effect is the same. I didn't *think* I was important to them, I didn't *feel* it.

We've begun to accept the sexual drives in us, we've begun (barely) to accept the *varieties* of sexual drives in us. I'm convinced the more we accept all of them, the more we fulfill all of them, the more powerful and efficient we'll become, the more fun and fulfillment—of all kinds—we'll get and the less of the Earth's resources we'll use to get them.

But we haven't begun, I think, to accept our ego needs—though we do a fair amount to gratify them. I think it'll be good when we do both: really gratify them, and acknowledge that we're gratifying them, acknowledge they're there. Acknowledge it to ourselves, which I don't think we do, and to others as well. Really revealing ourselves to others pays off big, I think (assuming the others want to be revealed to).

To continue the sex analogy, I don't think we're going to determine which sex drives are truly natural and healthy, assuming any aren't, until we've cleansed ourselves of the deeply embedded sex taboos we inherited from possibly millions of years and several species of predecessors who wouldn't have survived without the taboos. And only emotional work will accomplish this cleansing. Sex taboos are deeply embedded because they're deeply emotional. And they won't go away until we've fully experienced all the feelings that permeate them, nor until we've become reasonably proficient at meeting all our deepest needs, sex included. Even then some sex taboos might persist, which might assure their logical and eternal validity.

Same with ego. We won't know what kinds or components of ego are natural and healthy until we've cleansed ourselves of our outdated (although probably once necessary) bias against ego. A bias that makes so much of what we do to feed our egos covert, hidden, not only from others but, much worse, from ourselves. For example, I won't find out what's unhealthy in my egoism—what in it blocks achieving most fun, most fulfilling adaptation to my environment—until I experience all the feelings embedded in it and become a *lot* more proficient than I am now at meeting my deepest needs. Maybe I *need* to tell the world, or the part that'll listen, that I'm the Emperor.

My conviction, my faith, is that ego—the need, the drive, and the gratification and fulfillment of it—is all as beautiful a process and phenomenon as we're *beginning* to experience the sex process as being. The sex/love process. The ego process is *part* of the sex/love process, don't you think?

Hey, I don't dig arrogance either. Arrogance equals ego rape. It's a person who *hasn't* got what we commonly say he or she has: a "big ego." Arrogant people try to manipulate others into doing what they haven't been able to do themselves: convince themselves of how great they are. Hell, I think we're all great, stupefyingly so, it bends me toward belief in God when I think how great every *one* of us is—every human, every organism, every existent. The people who really know how great they are and who by a long shot don't need me to tell them, they're the winners who are going to save the world. The trick is to become one of them. Or at least to make sure the ones we bring in and raise are among them.

I'm one of them sometimes, I love myself a lot then and I think I then generate and amplify love around me. Love for me maybe, or just love, directed all over the place. That I'm not that all the time, not fully aware of how great I am and how much I can generate and amplify love around me, that I'm not that anywhere near enough of the time, is a big part of what's short in me.

Joan Goldberg believes that for her therapy to work, the client not only has to adopt Joan emotionally as a parent, but Joan has to adopt the client as her child. She has to love him or her that much, and if she doesn't think she's going to she won't take the person as a client. Freudians call this countertransference, and they categorically condemn it. Transference is when a client transfers to the psychotherapist the kinds of intense feelings he or she has had for important authority figures, like parents. This, Freudians believe, is vital to the success of psychoanalysis. But countertransference -- therapist becoming emotionally involved with client—is regarded as destructive in psychoanalysis and other psychotherapies.

Close the circle, insists Joan: two people embracing, not one embracing unreciprocated. And do it *only* when you feel it, when it comes from the core. Pretending, being nice—on the therapist's side say—is less than valueless.

So who's to blame for me? Parents? Didn't close the circle enough? You'll never catch me saying so. I'm nuts about my parents. They're in their 80s and alive in every imaginable way. I love them and—what I experience as the profounder and more potentially prized declaration—I know they love me. The circle is closed.

But some circles weren't. Thousands of circles I wanted closed weren't. Maybe if more of them were, I wouldn't need to be Emperor now.

Does everybody want to be Emperor, or something, and I'm the only one who's admitting it? Getting into it? Me and Donald Trump?

I don't know. But the faith that permeates every page of this book is that the *only* way to deal with such a need, such a desire is to get into it, All The Way. To feel it, experience it, surrender to the Emperor hunger when it bawls, oil the squeaky wheel, feed and fill the need the best you can. Fill the needs, feel the feelings. Emotional work.

That's the faith. If you don't want to do the faith, then don't do it. If you want to stay with the values of the old culture, the ones without which possibly several predecessor species over several millions of years would not have survived, a culture that might not be the "old" culture, that might very well be the only culture that will ever allow us to survive, now and for billions of years to come, if you want to do that, if you believe that, then do it. Believe it.

If you want to try this faith, even a little bit every once in a while, do it. Every instant of life is a gamble. Every move and not-move. You're an organism. Do your best as one. Think your way through, or, as I'm trying more and more to do, feel your way through. Use *all* your resources. Micro-move by micro-move, gamble by gamble. Go Simon!

DEDICATIONS

Stay with me, this'll be brief. To John Thorndike, a great novelist, for his immeasurable help on this book, and for his robust, malesome love whose value is enormous to me. To Joan Goldberg, a great therapist, thinker and experimenter, to Edith and Parks, I'll love them always, to Mom, Dad, my two brothers, their families, to all the family and friends I've been incredibly blessed with and whom I've grossly neglected while writing this essay.

Indeed to us all. To all us supremely great heroes and heroines, the individuals and species that preceded us, to the resourcefulness, wisdom and lust for life they embodied and that got us here, to us here now heroically addressing this peculiarly pivotal and hazardous time in our life system's evolution, to the ones who will inevitably follow regardless of what happens: I hope we do well by them, as well as we possibly can, as well as our forebears did by us.

To you. To me. To all us hero and heroine humans, primates, mammals, vertebrates, animals, organisms, existents, universes, antiuniverses, in all times, dimensions, past, present and future, a dedication: to us all. To The Emperor

Sandy Weymouth's dream, for most of his adult life, was to promote the cathartic experience of emotions: pain, rage, fear, joy, anything that comes up. He began his studies at the Casriel Institute in New York, and developed his own techniques and guidelines over a lifetime of practice. In his late forties he bought 23 acres of land in Maryland and established The Woods Place, a center devoted to exploring how all of us can best surrender to our feelings. Sandy died in 2014, but The Anthony E. Weymouth Foundation carries on his work.

www.ingramcontent.com/pod-product-compliance
Lightning Source LLC
Chambersburg PA
CBHW070959040426

42443CB00007B/572